WRITING ULSTER

WRITING ULSTER

NO 5
1998

AMERICA &
ULSTER

A CULTURAL CORRESPONDENCE

edited by
Bill Lazenbatt

and published by
The University of Ulster

Writing Ulster gratefully acknowledges the generous financial assistance of the Arts Council for Northern Ireland.

ACKNOWLEDGEMENTS

The editor wishes to thank Brandon Press for permission to publish Jenny Cornell's story 'Wax', which appears in the recent *Brandon Book of Irish Short Stories*. Thanks are also due to the artists of Seacourt Print Workshop and Texas Tech University, in particular David DuBose and Lynwood Krenick for permission to reproduce their work. The editor is also grateful to the Educational Development Unit of UUJ which provided support funding to train student editorial assistants as part of a wider educational initiative. Finally, thanks are due to Dunbar Design for their professionalism and invaluable assistance throughout the production of the journal. Every effort has been made to acknowledge ownership or copyright of materials used; any omissions are unintentional and, if brought to the attention of the editor, will gladly be corrected in the next issue.

The views expressed in this volume do not necessarily reflect those of the editor or publishers.

Editor: Bill Lazenbatt
Editorial Assistants: Janice Irvine
                       Anya Shields

Address for correspondence:

Writing Ulster, Room 12G11, University of Ulster at Jordanstown
Shore Road, Newtownabbey, Co Antrim, BT37 0QB, N. Ireland

TEL: 44 - 01232 - 366455
FAX: 44 - 01232 - 366824
e-mail: W.Lazenbatt@ulst.ac.uk

ISBN: 1 85923 102 0

Printed by ColourBooks

Designed by Dunbar Design

CONTENTS

EDITORIAL

Without recourse to *The Guinness Book of Records* – or even the Guinness itself! – I cannot remember exactly the number of United States presidents who claim ancestry from some part of Ireland, North or South. However, it is a significant number, and one which shows that the connection between Ulster and America is particularly strong in this respect. Historical links apart, there is also a cultural connection between the two places, which provides the subject matter for this edition of *Writing Ulster*.

Perhaps reciprocation is a better term to describe the sort of interaction which many of the following articles explore, and it is certainly a word which serves well to illustrate the generosity I allowed myself in selecting them: articles by Americans about Ulster, or about Ireland in general, are represented; as are articles by Ulster folk – and 'Ulster' university staff – about America. Expatriates find an opportunity to reflect on home, whether it be from the vantage points of Oregon, New Jersey or Dublin, and the reciprocal nature of cultural influence forms a common and wide-ranging theme throughout the collection.

From Oxford, Mississippi, Jane Mullen provides a novelist's perspective on Irish immigrant experience, while Matt McKee of Larne, County Antrim, looks somewhat sceptically at claims that Davy Crockett was of Ulster extraction. The Ulster poet, Frank Ormsby, evokes images of those 'Yanks' billeted here during the war, and records poetically one of their nostalgic return visits. Douglas Carson applies a particularly 'Ulster' form of wit to a tongue-in-cheek construction of a local family tree, and muses on the possibility that John Wayne might have ended up as Prime Minister of Northern Ireland! From the magic of the silver screen and the power of imagination, Sophie King mapped a childhood world to which she returns in her evocation of American film and its significance to her girlhood in Belfast, a significance which many of us will share wistfully as we recall those lost cinemas of youth. Representations of the harsher realisms of contemporary events in Ulster provide the images which Jenny Cornell analyses in her discussion of the Troubles and television drama, while her short story set in Belfast points to a more positive future. Music as a medium of cultural interaction does not go unnoticed, with essays on fiddle-playing by Hilary Bracefield and on Jazz influences on his own work by the celebrated Ulster poet, Michael Longley Back on 'Stateside', Maureen Murphy details the lives of Irish servant girls in the US as recorded in the literature of the nineteenth century, while Paul Muldoon spans the distance from the Moy to his life in Hopewell, with a New Englandly haiku. The Americanization of Ulster is further reflected in Lee Wright's discussion of design features in the province, while Jerushia McCormack looks more sceptically at the same process as it affects Irish life in general.

One of my favourite anecdotes is of the pedantic and long-winded English grammarian who bores his US audience by belabouring the fact that the double negative produces a positive; it is not however the case, he pontificates, that a double positive produces a negative. 'Yeah, yeah!' responds the laconic American in the front row! If our two cultures are indeed separated by the use of a common language, I have decided on an editorial largesse which welcomes variety, even in such serious matters as punctuation. I have consciously therefore not 'standardized' spellings and constructions from one article to the next. Let eagle-eyed detractors mutter imprecations if they will, like a transatlantic Walt Whitman the spirit of *Writing Ulster* is large and can contain multitudes!

The high quality and subtle dual reference of our cover deserves one final comment, since it visually represents both sides of the cultural alliance I have been suggesting. The image is a composite of works by Ulster artist Gail Kelly and her Texan husband, David DuBose. From their base in Bangor, Co Down, where David is Manager of the

Seacourt Print Workshop, they collaborated last year with Lynwood Kreneck of Texas Tech University in Lubbock in presenting a simultaneous exchange exhibition of original prints. This meant that the public who visited Belfast's Waterfront Hall during the exhibition viewed a selection of prints from Texas and from Ulster which was exactly the same display presented in Lubbock at exactly the same time. *Writing Ulster* was fortunate in gaining permission to reproduce a number of the prints in this issue, for which we thank all of the artists concerned. The cover combines David's use of strong colour with Gail's more muted shades in the dolmen-like rocks to produce an image which suggests just how effective a cultural alliance between Ulster and the US can be. That is the general belief which informs this edition and one which I hope you will discover and enjoy in the articles which follow.

BILL LAZENBATT

Malainn Mhor

GAIL KELLY

ALL THE OLD SONGS

JANE MULLEN

MARY ELLEN

What was it like there? Not what he was thinking. No. But what did she know of her country? She was fifteen when she left. She could tell him only about her own family, her own village. Oh, there was bad times enough, to be sure, and plenty of talk to be heard of when there was nothing to eat, only grass and seaweed. Her own grandmother would tell how she lost her whole family to the famine and the fever until there was only herself and her mother left. Then the mother died and she, a girl of twenty-three, had to shoulder her to the graveyard. There was neither sheet nor coffin to cover the dead and she had only a handkerchief to lay over her mother's face so the earth wouldn't be shoveled straight onto it. Everyone had a story like that to tell, and tell them they did. But Mary Ellen had never known hunger, and even her grandmother, who lived on another forty years after burying her mother, ended her days between white sheets with a loaf roasting in the fire.

Their farm was at the foot of a great hill, steep and broad and covered in their seasons with heather and gorse. The hill was for the cows and below was the meadow for hay and the tillage for oats and potatoes, cabbages and turnips. On the crest of the hill was a ring of old stones, each as tall as a man, it was said had been there a thousand years. The ring was too high up to be seen from the farm below, but if you were coming from over the top of the hill beyond, there it was across the valley, a great circle of stones like a giant's crown set on the head of their own hill, and the sight of it would shake the soul in you for thinking how it had come to be there.

2

Their house was straight at the foot of that hill and built into it for shelter, no windows at the back. Three good rooms with a thatch roof the hens would be laying their eggs in if you didn't keep after them, and then you would have a time getting the eggs down, and the hens would be scratching holes in the thatch that would let in the rain. No, you had to keep the hens out of the thatch. The house was warm and dry inside no matter how wet the day because of the fire that had never been let go out as long as she could remember. At night the ashes would be raked over and in the morning the live embers stirred up again and a fresh sod or two put on. It was her mother saw to the fire and when she died it was Johanna. Johanna was the oldest girl, the one her own Johanna was called for. Mary Ellen was the youngest; five sisters she had, and one brother. Tom. No son of hers was called after him.

Nine of them there were. Ten, when her grandmother was alive. You try to feed that many people on a working man's pay in the city of Boston and they will starve. But theirs was a good farm and they had their own eggs and milk and butter, potatoes, cabbages, turnips. They had rabbit, bacon, a hen now and then. There was little enough money, but what was the need for it? Tea and tobacco, sugar. Nearly every half-crown that came into the house was put by to dower whichever one of the girls would be the first to get the offer of a decent farm to marry into.

Nine. But there was none of this moaning about one more mouth to feed. That was something you never heard there. Seven children meant seven helping hands. Tom had the most of it. He worked with her father cutting the turf, helping with the calving and the sowing and the seeding and the plowing, with manuring the potatoes, with putting them down in the spring and digging them up in the summer. The girls did the washing, milking, churning. Feed the hens, fetch the water, go to the hill to bring down the cows, go for the turf. And the haying. They all helped with the haying.

Evenings some of the neighbors would be coming in and some of their own would be going out, especially in the winter. Winter nights were long with darkness falling well before the evening meal was taken.

A neighbor would come in at the door and take a seat. Then another would come, then another, and soon they'd be puffing their pipes and someone would begin telling about something that had happened to him that day, or something he'd seen or heard, and when he was good and finished with his telling, another would say how that minded him of something, and one story would lead to another until the long night was shortened to its end.

3

It wasn't like here: work all day and fall into bed, crawl out of the bed and work all day. There the work was only for the life. The life wasn't only for the work. Nights were not for bracing yourself to work again. Night was the time for rambling, going to the houses where there was talk or cards or music, sometimes even dancing. Until two and three and even four in the morning they would be going in and out of each other's houses. In the pitch dark and with distances to travel, people would be up and down the roads all night. Francis Colleran was now going to work at the same time he used to be going to his bed. The cows and the hens didn't dock a man for getting his sleep in.

It was mostly the old men like her father who came to their house in the evenings. The women would go to another house, the young men to another for their cards. That was how it was done. There was a great distance kept between the men and the women. Her sisters would go out when the men started coming in. But her mother never liked to leave her own hearth. She'd sit with her bit of knitting and Mary Ellen would sit by her, her own two hands idle, trying to keep her eyes open until her mother would be called for a song.

Her mother never refused. She might ask for a swallow of water, but then she would lay down her work and with no fuss begin to sing. She never had to be coaxed. God did not give you a light to hide it under your cloak, she would say. The men would look at the floor but would follow each note with a nod of their heads, and Mary Ellen would imagine herself the girl in the song, the one left under the sod by the heart-broken husband, the one shedding tears on the grass over his head, or the one whose true love was on the dark ocean.

Why did she leave? She didn't want to. She didn't want to go from her home, leave alone her country. America had no lure for her. Some

had returned with money they'd earned in the factories and they had different clothes for every Sunday in the month. But what were fine clothes on a girl who'd lost the bloom in her cheek and the light in her eye, her health gone from the hard work and the bad air? No, she had no wish to go. Few did want to go, but few could stay.

This was how it was. A mother and father who had seven children had fourteen hands to help with the work, but when the mother and father grew old or died, what was to happen to the six who did not get the farm? Tom would get the farm. He was provided for. The dowry his wife would bring to his father would dower one of the girls. The money their father was saving would dower one more. That was three of seven. The rest must travel. That was the way of it. A girl did not marry without a dowry. A boy did not marry until he got the farm.

Mary Ellen was only a child. All that should have been years off from her. But everything changed when her mother died. Her father cared for nothing after her. He turned his face to the way she had gone and he'd no heart for the work anymore. Tom was only twenty-six, but he wanted to marry. He wanted their father to turn the farm over to him, and their father was ready to do it. It was good land and a good house and would bring in a good dowry. But what woman would come into a house with six unmarried girls in it? So when a man with a better farm than his offered to take one of his daughters for nothing, it seemed an answer to her father's prayers, and to refuse the offer a slap in the face of God Himself. John Garvan had no father to demand a dowry and no sister to be provided for. His old mother died and he could do what he pleased, and it pleased him to say he would take Mary Ellen Kearney without a penny.

She was asleep when there came a knock at the door. She heard men's voices and then her father's. Then Tom went out to talk with them. They talked on and on and from time to time there'd be the sound of a bottle and cup. Mary Ellen was drifting in and out of sleep, but her sisters were straining to hear. They all knew a match was being made. They didn't know would it be Johanna or Susan or Norah or Mairead, or even Rose, who was being spoken for. None of them thought it would be Mary Ellen. It was not heard of for a girl with five older sis-

ters to marry so young. There was five years between herself and Rose because of all the children their mother had lost in between. She was only fifteen. Most girls were twenty before they married, or even thirty. A boy could be forty or fifty before his father was in the grave or made over the land to him. Johanna was twenty-seven. It should have been her.

When their father came into the room and said Mary Ellen was to put on her clothes, Johanna told him to let the child get her sleep. She would put a drop of water on the fire if it was a cup of tea they were wanting. It's Mary Ellen that's wanted, he said, and make no mistake about it.

Johanna had to help her get her arms into her clothes and push her out of the room, she was that asleep. There were six men, counting her father and brother, sitting round the hearth smoking their pipes, and her heart was broken when she saw John Garvan among them, for it was well known he'd be in want of a wife now that his old mother was dead. There was joking about him among the girls, that he'd be getting himself a wife now his mother was gone and he'd no one to milk the cows. He'd not had the courage to bring in another woman over his shrew of a mother, and now he was fifty if he was a day.

Her father asked what did she think of going to the richest farm in the townland. He asked her three times, but she could say nothing at all. He put his fist under her chin and raised her head. Well? Out with your tongue, if you please. She said she was not ready to marry. She said she wanted to learn a bit more first. You'd be better off with a bit of sense, my girl, her father said, and sent her back to bed.

That should have been the end of it. It wasn't usual for a girl to be forced to marry against her will. If a man didn't suit, she'd only to say so. But that was rare. Most girls were glad of the chance of a husband and a house of their own. Any one of her sisters would have willingly tied the knot with John Garvan, old as he was. Her father had said no more than the truth when he'd spoken of the richest farm in the townland. The Garvans' crops never failed, their animals never sickened and died, their milk never turned, their butter was sweet, their house clean and white-washed. They even had a separate house for the animals.

But she was too young, and he was too old. Too old and as much to look at as that old stove. And he had no talk. All those nights, listening to the men, she'd noticed he hadn't a spare word to throw to a dog. But if she'd hoped that would be the end of it, she was mistaken. Her father was still sitting staring into the fire when she finally got up again. Johanna looked at her and then quick back to her work. The way her father started right in on her she knew he'd been sitting there just waiting for her to put her head through the door. Wasn't she the grand lady that morning who thought she'd maybe marry a duke or a king the way she was after refusing a fortune for herself and a bit of comfort for himself in his last days?

And this was another thing. John Garvan, having no old people of his own, was offering to put her father into the room his mother had died out of. Her father would have his own daughter as mistress of the house and not a strange daughter-in-law who would maybe talk back to him or even put him out on the road altogether.

He kept on at her, but she said nothing and Johanna kept silent as well. They knew there was no use talking to him when he had a drop on board. The best thing was to let him talk himself out and then sleep it off. But while he was still ranting, Tom came in from the haggard and started in on her too, even though Johanna kept looking daggers at him. Where was he to find a wife would come into a house full of girls, especially with one as young as herself in it who'd be ten years before she got another offer? Hadn't she a thought or a care for anyone but herself? How was he to rid himself of a houseful of useless women and get a wife would give him some sons that would be of some help to him if those who were offered decent opportunities turned them down? And her father was chiming in saying if Tom didn't marry their name would die out and the land revert to the sheep or to strangers.

Even so, she might have been let be if the priest hadn't come into it. There wasn't much the priest didn't have a hand in, a sickness or a death, a birth or a funeral, a marriage or a match. Maybe that was why so many things were settled between the night and the morning. To keep the priest out of them. But John Garvan was first cousin to the priest and went straight to him with the news that Mary Ellen Kearney

had refused his offer. The priest came to see her father that same day. But it wasn't John Garvan he wanted married. It was herself. A pretty girl was seen by him as nothing but an occasion of sin, nothing but a temptation, something to be got rid of before it became the cause of an offense to God, like you'd hear you should cut off your right hand if you thought you'd maybe do something sinful with it.

7

This was not to speak ill of all priests. Before that one was sent to them they'd had one who was kind and good and generous and wise. Because there were good ones and bad ones. But no matter what they were, the people were at their mercy, and that was one difference between that country and this. If Father Cleary were to come up those stairs and swing his stick at their heads because they were found talking together, they could go down to the police precinct and swear out a warrant against him. But there. There you would jump out the door and hope he didn't catch you or recognize you or read you from the altar next Sunday morning.

She'd said there was a great distance kept between the men and the women and that was the truth. The boys would walk on one side of the road and the girls on the other. The women would sit in one half of the church and the men in the other or stand at the back. But the boys and girls found ways of getting to know each other just the same. They'd even had a dance or two in one of the houses. Mary Ellen had got to know both Tomas and Robert Brennan, who were cousins, and who got into an argument because of her, because first she was talking to one and then she was talking to the other. She said she wouldn't talk to either of them if they didn't cool their tempers, and so they did. But later that night walking home Robert got his teeth knocked down his throat, and the next day his brother was laying for Tomas after Mass and half killed him.

It was just two days after that when John Garvan told the priest Mary Ellen had refused his offer. The priest went straight to her father and told him in no uncertain terms to see that she accepted the offer. He said that the sooner she was married the better for everyone, and he told him there had already been two fights because of her. Her sisters all stood by her, and her father might have listened to them, especially

to Johanna. But the pleading of a hundred sisters is only a feather in the wind against the word of a priest. Her father told her she would take John Garvan and that was the end of it. He and Tom took a bottle to him and drank on it and a date was set. She was to be married the following Tuesday.

She lost two days crying her eyes out but never thinking anything other than the deed was done. It wasn't until the third day she decided to set her heels to the road. When everyone else was out of the house she went to the tin box and took out all the money. She didn't even look to see how much it was. It wouldn't have meant anything to her if she had; she had never bought anything. She took it all, not knowing how much she would need. She put it inside her clothes, then went down to the well to get water for the washing.

Next morning, long before anyone else would be thinking of rising from their beds, she put on her Sunday clothes and then her other ones on top of them. She was trying not to make a sound, carrying her shoes and not even breathing. When she moved past where Johanna was sleeping, her sister reached out and took hold of her arm, giving her such a fright she nearly called out. But it was not to stop her. Johanna pulled her down to the bed, took her head in her two hands and kissed her lips, then gave her a little push, and off she was, out the door, never looking back, never stopping, not even to put on her boots, until she was on the other side of the valley.

There'd been others gone from the village before her. She was only a young child when Francis Colleran emigrated, but she well remembered the wake they'd given him. American wakes they were called, because those leaving were as good as dead to those left behind, except for the money they'd be sending from beyond the grave. People came from all over the townland. There was singing and dancing and eating and drinking and talking and laughing and weeping. It went on all the night. No such thing as resting up for the journey. And in the morning they walked with him part of the way across the valley, then stopped and let him go on alone, watching until he reached the top of the hill beyond, where he turned and waved his hat. And the whole village lifted their hands in farewell, his mother and sisters crying out his

8

name long after he'd gone from their sight.

But when she turned that morning for a last look there was not a soul to be seen, so what she carried in her eyes still was the last glimpse of the house across the valley where she was reared, and the first light of day striking the ring of stones on the top of her father's hill.

She was two days getting to the city of Cork and then out to Queenstown where the ships sailed from, walking mostly, asking whenever she dared which was the way to America, and then the last hours by train. She thought people just went to the harbour, got on a boat, and sailed away, but there was more to it than that. She had to find a shipping agent and tell lie after lie. You had to give your name and age and occupation. You had to say how much money you had in your possession. You had to give the address you were coming from and the one you were going to. Nothing was checked on that end. They didn't care. It was just a matter of filling out their forms. But she didn't know that. She was terrified of being found out.

And she had to wait another four days, had to look for lodgings. She walked up and down the quays, such a big, bustling, confusing place with the harbor full of ships and boats and the town full of houses, hundreds and hundreds of houses in every color of the rainbow built shoulder to shoulder in rank upon rank and tier upon tier all the way up to the top of the cliffside, and the sky above alive with the flapping and screeching and swooping of white gulls. She walked all day before she got up the courage to knock on a door and ask for a bed. Then once inside, where she had to tell a whole new set of lies, she was afraid to go out again, afraid of being recognized and caught. She thought the day would never come, she thought she would not be able to breathe free until her ship would have turned its stern to the shore.

And that ship. It was nothing like the ships she'd seen pictures of, wooden vessels with yards and yards of sails. Her ship was made of iron and steel and gave out great blasts of steam from its black chimneys, its name in white letters, each the size of a human child, stretching the length of the bows. She was so eager to be off, she was one of the first up the gangway when the restraining ropes were let down. But the second a blast went out from the ship's horn, the second it began to back and to turn, such a lamentation rose from the people crowding the decks and the people crowding the quays, such wailing and weeping as she had thought could only be heard from the souls in hell, that she was filled with terror for what she had done, and when the doors of a church on the hill high over the harbor swung open and a crowd of people came spilling out into the sunshine, she would have jumped overboard if she had known how to swim. But the ship kept moving and turning until there was nothing ahead of them but the long grey edge of the sky.

That's when he saw her, when he spoke to her. He was one of the ones herding the steerage passengers along their descent. He was kind to her. He spoke the first kind words she'd heard in days, the first words not full of suspicion and censure. He steered her along. He showed her where to go, showed her her bunk.

There was no privacy. There were two hundred people in her section and they were separated from the other sections by short wooden fences, just horizontal boards with wide spaces between. There was one washroom used by both the men and the women, one faucet of cold salt water. The berths had straw mattresses and no pillows and were stacked in tiers with only low partitions between them. There was no baggage space, no place to dress, no buckets for seasickness. And everybody was sick. It was a rough passage, a terrible passage full of terrible spring storms with heavy rains and mountainous waves. There was no escape from the sounds of people throwing up and groaning and cursing, from the children crying and the women shrieking, no escape from the stench or from being slammed against each other with the rising and sinking of the ship.

He came to her whenever he could, always bringing her something: clean bread, a cup of fresh water, a mug of tea, a pillow, a blanket, salts to help with the seasickness. He would take her to where she could get a mouthful of air, his arm tight around her waist to keep her from falling with the pitching of the ship. She clung to him. He was all she had in the world.

She didn't know his name, where he was from or even which country he lived in. She thought he must be English, but wasn't sure.

There was very little talking. He wasn't supposed to be anywhere near her. It was always a matter of sneaking and silence and secrecy, of keeping out of the way, out of sight, and when they were alone in the place where he took her for air, they had to shout above the howling of the wind and the crashing of the sea. She was petrified they were all going to drown and she wanted nothing more than his arms tight around her, pressing her close to him for protection and comfort. He did not force her. She wanted to be taken out of the hell of the present and the terror of the future and to exist only in that exact moment of time.

She thought, if she thought at all, that she loved him and that he loved her. She never doubted that, if they lived, he would take care of her. But she was sure they would die, that she would sink in his arms to the bottom of the sea. She never thought she would leave that ship, never suspected that when she did, when the grey headlands of Boston harbour appeared through the fog and the time came for her to disembark, to be examined and tagged and put in a pen and turned over to the droves of waiting schemers and hustlers, he would simply fade into the background and disappear from her life.

And so. That was why she had come to America.

That was why she soon found herself in need of the protection offered her by Francis Colleran, a man whose name, if not his face, she remembered from when she was a child, a kind man, a good man, a man not two years younger than old John Garvan.

That was why Frank, who must never know, looked more like an English sailor than he did his own father.

And that was why the pennies would be placed on her eyes before she would see the green land of Ireland again.

FRANK

After Frank came Johanna, then Owen. There was also Rose and Brian, but Brian died of pneumonia and Rose of scarlet fever. When Rose got sick the others had to wear yellow arm bands to mark them as carriers, and when she died their flat was fumigated by the Board of Health. For years, until his best friend at school died of it, Frank thought scarlet fever was a family disease and had a red name because Rose was a red name. Later he would have two more brothers, Ned and Sam, Jr. But in 1908, when Frank was twelve, there was just himself and Johanna and Owen. His mother sang.

Farewell to you, hills and green valleys ...

She used to sing him to sleep, then she used to sing the others to sleep. now she sang while she sewed. Before the Sullivans, there'd been a Jewish family from Poland downstairs. Frank's mother would light their stove and oil lamp every Sabbath because it was too bad for them to have to sit in the dark and the cold, and in return the woman taught Frank's mother how to sew. She sewed all the time. Johanna had three different dresses and their father four shirts. Their father said he had so many clothes now he didn't know where to put them. But mostly she sewed for other people, for the other Irish women who didn't like going to foreigners for anything. She made nightgowns and chemises and shirtwaists with long flowing sleeves, and skirts that were supposed to sweep the pavement but were cut to ankle-length to keep them out of the dirt and the mud and the horse manure that fell to the streets of Boston at the rate of a hundred and thirty tons a day.

all this beauty I'm leaving ... I'm bound for a distant land ...

On dark winter days with the kitchen windows stuffed with news-papers and rags to keep out the wind that came howling across the frozen harbor, his mother would sing about mountain streams, morn-ings breaking fresh and fair, the sun on the waves of Lough Shoolin, a green glade in Agadoe. She sang in a high, haunting voice, thin as a razor's edge and sharp as a needle that cut right through Frank and filled him with a wild lonesomeness. Sometimes when he looked up

she'd be sitting perfectly still, her back straight as any Protestant's, the sewing forgotten in her lap, her eyes fixed on another time and place, and he would be jealous.

He was jealous of that distant land where his mother had lived without him, where she could take herself anytime she wanted, and his father, too. He would let his newspaper sag and he would go with her, just like that, leaving Frank behind, leaving him and Johanna and Owen behind in their kitchen in another country. Frank wanted more than anything in the world for his mother to forget that place, so he never asked her a single question about it, and when she would try to talk about it, when she would say that this reminded her of the time when her father … or that reminded her of when her sister Johanna … he would not say anything, unless it was to correct her. Because she never said she remembered something, she said she minded it.

I mind the time Johanna and myself …

Don't say that, Frank would beg her. It's Johanna and I. I remember the time Johanna and I …

He wanted her to be an American. He was an American. His sister and brother were Americans. It killed him that his mother wasn't and didn't even seem to want to be. He wanted her to sing *She Lives in Alabama* and *Meet Me in St. Louis*. He was always humming or whistling the tunes he'd picked up in the streets where they'd drifted from the music halls and the theatres and the composing rooms of Tin Pan Alley. But she never caught on. She sang only the old songs, the songs she'd brought with her in the time before Frank was born.

They lived in a four-family rowhouse on a street of four-family rowhouses in a neighborhood of four-family rowhouses in Boston's South End, which had been emptied of its old Yankee owners, who had lived only one family to each house, and filled with not just four times but ten times as many new people, immigrants from all over Europe, whose large families overflowed into the hallways and down the dark stairways and spilled out into the narrow and crooked streets full of horse dung and rotting vegetables, pushcarts and sour pickle stands.

Their flat was on the second floor, five small rooms his father had furnished at the start with lean mattresses on iron frames, a cupboard,

a kitchen table, some wooden chairs and kerosene lamps. They shared a privy with upwards of thirty other people, a clothesline, and a stingy patch of sky over a fenced-in dirt yard. In the kitchen was a small sink for washing dishes and a square tub for washing themselves and their clothes, and a round black stove, the only source of heat in the flat, which was freezing in the winter and suffocating in the summer. Frank's father took care of shoveling coal into their bin in the cellar, but until Frank started selling newspapers, he was the one to bring the bucket of coal up to the kitchen first thing every morning, a job he hated even more than his summer chore of lugging their block of ice all the way from the corner at Harrison, where the wagon stopped for their street.

Now Johanna and Owen had to take turns bringing up the coal, since Frank had to get up at five-thirty to get to Newspaper Row, pick up his papers, peddle every last one of them, and get home again to hand over his pennies and eat some breakfast before going to school. Johanna hated getting the coal even more than Frank had; the noise of the shovel going into it set her teeth on edge, and she kept having the same dream about a tramp hiding in the cellar. Owen was so spooked by the cellar that five times out of ten he'd drop the key to the pad-locked bin, and while he felt around the floor for it, his candle would go out and he'd start howling.

They complained loudly about these things, but Frank at least could see they were lucky. They had to contribute their share, they had their chores, but there were lots of boys he knew, and girls too, who were working, who'd had to leave school and go to work when their fathers got sick or died, when they were kicked by a horse, lost an arm or a leg in a machine, slipped from a shaky scaffold or were crushed by a load of iron or steel falling on them. Or they were fired or laid off or drank their pay or couldn't find a job in the first place, like Jimmy Riley's father who had only one eye because he'd lost the other one looking for work. Looking too damn hard, he would say, when he had a drop in him.

Frank's father used to work in the box factory, then he worked at the Navy Yard, now he worked for a contractor digging sewers and haul-

ing dirt from construction sites. His mother could go into Jacobson's grocery herself and hold her head up and pay cash for what she bought, even if it was only beans and potatoes and tea, milk poured into their jug from the rusty cans at the front of the store, and strong-smelling yellow butter carefully weighed out by the ounce, as if it were gold. Lots of families he knew sent one of the children to ask for food on credit despite the WE SELL FOR CASH ONLY: NO CREDIT sign big as a circus poster in the window. Mr. Jacobson wouldn't let anybody in the neighborhood starve, but Frank would see Mary Slaney, Johanna's best friend, coming home from his store, her face burning with shame from the tongue-lashing he'd given her (Beggars! Oh, these beggars!), trying to hide the bread under her coat so Frank wouldn't see it was only half a loaf of pumpernickel.

When his mother did send him to the store for a tin of sardines for a Saturday treat for his father, she always gave him the four cents to pay for it. If anyone had told Frank that his family was poor, it would have been news to him. He thought they were pretty well off. Enough to eat and good enough clothes. Five rooms to themselves when there were families of ten and eleven and twelve washing, cooking, eating and sleeping in two or three rooms. And people were always moving out because they couldn't pay the rent; every other flat in Frank's building had turned over three or four times. But his family never had to move. Their three and a half dollars rent was always ready on Saturday morning when Mr. Chase came to collect it. They knew when he was coming because they would hear him pounding on the door downstairs and shouting at the Sullivans to open up or be served first thing Monday with a notice of eviction. Frank's mother would count out the money from the box, where his father had put every last cent of his pay the night before, and tell Frank to give it to Mr. Chase, a small black-eyed man with a thin moustache and pointed beard, who was always looking over Frank's shoulder, looking for his mother. But his mother kept out of sight until she heard the landlord banging on the Nolans' door upstairs.

His mother had eyes the same blue as the October sky and hair black as the coal. It embarrassed Frank that she was always looked at, and

looked at a second time, but he was glad she hadn't grown into one of those bloated, red-faced, coarse-looking and worse-talking women like those who lived all around them. Sometimes he thought that was why his father didn't beat her and why he didn't drink. Other times he thought it was the other way round, that his mother stayed pretty because his father was good to her, because he worshipped her instead of horsewhipped her. And his mother loved his father, too.

She did. She did. Frank knew she did.

Look at when his father was killed, when the subway tunnel he was digging collapsed, when he was carried up the stairs and laid just as he was on the bed, his mother went down on her knees, stretched her arms across him, and let out a wail that lifted the hair on their necks. She spoke to him, though he was clearly dead, she begged and beseeched him not to leave her with four young children and no way to put bread in their mouths. How was she to live on after him, night following night and he never coming in through the door? Her heart's darling, she called him. Her heart's only love. Francis, don't leave her. Francis, don't go. She called his name again and again. Francis, Francis.

Her cries rose and fell like waves all around them until old Mrs. Whealon finally got herself up the stairs and threw open the window so their father's spirit could escape. Then came the priest, red-faced Father Cleary with the rough tongue of a cat. Shame, shame, shame. Such carrying on in the face of God's will. And in front of those poor youngsters. It was to his eternal reward their father had been called; that was how they must be taught to think, and through her own example. She got to her feet and looked down at Frank's father. Dirt filled his eyes and his mouth; his broken nails were clotted with blood. Her voice was quiet now.

Reward? It's a poor enough reward has been in store for Francis Colleran this long while, and he not knowing.

She snatched up her shawl and draped it across the mirror over the dresser. She tried to stop the hands of the wind-up clock, and when she could not get at them, she took it to the kitchen and smashed the glass with the meat mallet, then she turned the shaving mirror to the wall.

She loved him. She did.

Other mothers came in all the time weeping and cursing and telling how this one had been knocked to the floor, that one thrown down the steps with the baby in her arms, the other locked out in the street on a bitter winter night. This husband had drunk his pay or that one sentenced to a month on Deer Island for disorderly conduct, leaving his family to starve. Frank's mother always sent him out of the kitchen but he heard enough. Just lying in bed on airless summer nights he heard the arguing and bickering coming through the open window of the little room off the kitchen he shared with Owen. Just walking down the street, any street, he'd hear a man shouting or a woman screaming above the clanging and screeching of the trolley cars and the sharp staccato of the horses' hoofs striking sparks out of the cobblestones.

There were fathers who wouldn't walk the length of the block with their own wives or children, who would consider it a disgrace to their manhood to be seen walking in broad daylight with any woman, let alone a wife. But Frank's father went to church with them every Sunday, walking beside Frank's mother, Johanna and Owen following them to the white granite church at the corner of Harrison and Concord, where Frank would already be selling his papers to the people coming out of the nine o'clock mass. Afterwards his mother and Johanna got the dinner while his father read the news and Frank and Owen read the funnies. *Happy Hooligan, The Captain and The Kids, Buster Brown.* There were eight pages of them; you could spend the whole afternoon at it, especially when you had to keep explaining to Owen what was so funny.

Owen was eight years old and never seemed to understand anything, but Frank was smart and did well in school, not only because on any given day he was able to give his teachers back a good portion of the information they'd hammered into him the day before, but because he really believed both their threats and their promises. Lazy, sloppy, disobedient children would come to a bad end. Those who possessed a good character and worked hard would be rewarded. If a child had to have his character beaten into him, then so be it; it was all for his own good. Frank's father had set the tone on Frank's first day of school, when he left him at the door of Joshua Bates Elementary with the caution never to come home whining about having been given a thrashing by a teacher, or he'd be given another one, and one he'd not soon forget.

But the only real thrashing Frank had ever been given he paid back-with so much interest that he'd cost the other boy his hearing in one ear and had never been challenged again, not even by Roberto Ruggio, who was so fearless he'd once thrown an inkwell straight at a teacher's face. At twelve, Frank already had a reputation as one of the best batters in the South End, a really savage line-drive hitter. A good-looking boy with blond hair and grey eyes, stocky and thick-set and tall enough to carry it off, he was already head and shoulders over his mother and had even passed his father, a small, compact man with close-set eyes. Where Frank's height and strong build had come from was a mystery to the neighbor women, even though his mother always said he'd gotten his strength straight from the hand of God. Whatever its source, it was a distinct advantage to a boy who had to be out in the streets every morning hours before the sun was even thinking of rising.

He never knew what he'd come across. Of the seven thousand drunks arrested in the South End every year, he saw a fair number, weaving their lost way homeward or still lying where they'd fallen after being thrown out the side door of a saloon. He wasn't afraid of them. They were rag dolls, marionettes, limbs jerked this way and that by some malicious unseen prankster. Frank knew he was equal to any drunk. What frightened him were his occasional confrontations with women, ladies of the night he came to think of them, all on his own.

Once, he crossed a street and stepped right into the path of two young women. They seized him, knocked off his cap, ruffled his hair, enveloped him in their dusky perfume. For him, just a dime, said the dark one; he was an angel. Two for a dime, the redhead offered, taking hold of his chin and looking into his eyes, coaxing. Just a nickel? He had no idea what these women were selling, but they terrified him. They turned him to water. They turned him soft and hard all at the same time, then suddenly turned him loose and walked off away, their throaty voices raised in blasphemous song. *Next to Your Mother, Who Do You Love?* Since then, whenever he heard female laughter or deter-

mined heels clacking sharply on the pavement, he'd duck down an areaway or into a side street or head for the yellow flame from the torch of an early-morning pushcart setting up to sell hot roast potatoes to hungry men on their way to work.

One bitter March morning he went outside at six o'clock and found a drunk half-frozen to the bottom step. He gave the man a wide berth and sprinted down the street. If the tramp was still there when he got back, he'd do something, tell somebody. But there was something about the way the long, inert flgure lay there dusted with snow that made Frank go and take another look. It was starting to snow seriously, the mercury dropping fast, a real nor'easter blowing in. The man wouldn't have a snowball's chance in hell if he stayed there another two hours, if he wasn't already dead. Frank didn't want to get close enough to find out. He went back upstairs for his father. They could at least carry the bum in out of the snow and lay him on the floor of the hallway until he sobered up. Which is what they did, and five minutes later Frank was on his way again, feeling good enough about himself.

But when he came back from selling his papers, covered with snow and half frozen himself, he wasn't all that happy to find the drunk had been brought up to their kitchen and laid across four chairs pushed together; his mother pointed out they might as well have left him out in the snow as leave him to freeze to death down in the hallway. Frank ate his oatmeal standing up, since Johanna and Owen already had the other two chairs, and took in the tramp's bushy beard, harboring God only knew what manner of vermin, the red eyelids and cracked lips, the long black boots broken open at the sides and too-short jacket gone at the elbows, the newspapers stuffed inside the buttonless shirt, the piece of dirty red flannel knotted at the unwashed neck.

The doctor had been sent for, his mother told him; his father had called in on his way to work. It wasn't a question of drink. There was no smell of drink off the man.

On him, Frank insisted. No smell of drink on him.

What in the name of God had gotten into Frank, his mother wanted to know. It wasn't like him to bite the head off his own mam.

Frank never called his mother mam.

When he came home from school he saw that the filthy clothes had been exchanged for one of his father's clean nightshirts and the tramp's long, thin form installed in Frank's own bed, which had been moved out of the little room off the kitchen and set up near the stove. Who had done this? Who had removed the man's clothes? Surely not his mother.

Dr. Scanlon had said it was pneumonia, she told him; he'd said they might as well put a bullet through the poor soul's head as move him. They had taken Frank's bed because Owen's cot was too small for the great length of the man. She would make up a bed for Frank on the kitchen chairs that night. He'd be right near the stove and warm as toast. He was a good boy, Frank was.

He didn't have to ask why they were doing this for a complete stranger. He thought he knew why. He thought it was because she too believed all the threats and the promises, because she believed it was entirely possible for Christ to come to your door disguised as a tramp or a beggar, and you turned him away at the cost of your immortal soul, and took him in to your eternal credit. There had been other times. They had once had an evicted family of seven living in the front room for two weeks.

This time it was seventeen days, seventeen nights that Frank slept on a make-shift bed of kitchen chairs tied together with rags to keep them from pushing apart and lined with seat cushions from the parlor sofa and chairs, an arrangement he refused to admit was pretty snug. Dr. Scanlon said more than once this was a very sick man they had on their hands and that now the weather had settled he ought to be moved over to the hospital. But that's what he had said about Frank's brother Brian, and Brian had never come out again. Frank's mother had seen too many people go into the charity ward, never to return. She continued to nurse the scabby stranger with a determination Frank knew had something to do with Brian and Rose. She fed him beef tea spoonful by spoonful, applied and changed hot reeking mustard plasters, coaxed him through one raving, sweating crisis after another. And she sang.

Farewell to you ...

The man never spoke, no matter what was asked, no matter what was

said to him, he never indicated by so much as a nod or a shake of the head that he understood a word. They thought he must be a Swede or a Lithuanian, or even a Frog, since neighbors had tried German, Italian and Polish on him to no avail. One thing was clear, Frank's father said. The man hadn't a word of English in his mouth, so it was no use wearing out their tongues talking to him. And just as well.

21

The whole family practically lived in the kitchen in the winter. They not only ate there, the children played and fought and did their memorizing there, their mother cooked and washed and sewed, their father read the paper. The parlor with its horsehair sofa and chairs bought on the two-dollar-a-month installment plan was not meant to be used by the family, who viewed it chiefly from the doorway. It was reserved for a special occasion, a wedding or a wake, although in winter it was convenient to store the pot of leftover soup or stew in there, or the Sunday piece of meat, which had to be taken out and thawed hours ahead of time, it was that cold. The bedrooms were just as bad. The family could sleep in them if they kept their heads under the blankets, but they couldn't get into their clothes anywhere but in the kitchen, where Frank's father had constructed a kind of screen from a dresser and a cupboard pushed together at right angles. They were already so confined it would have been a hardship if they thought, if they knew, this stranger was hearing every word they said.

On the morning of the third Saturday the man lay in their kitchen, Johanna and Owen went out to play in the first real spring weather. Frank had just given the landlord his three dollars and fifty cents and was going out himself to try to get up a baseball game on the empty lot on Canton Street. Only he didn't want to leave his mother alone with this man who followed her with his eyes whenever he thought no one was watching him. He looked guilty somehow, like a man with an uneasy conscience, and even though he was too weak to harm a blind kitten, Frank did not trust him.

And he was right, it seemed, his suspicions were well-founded, because when he changed his mind about playing baseball and went back upstairs, back into the kitchen, Frank found the man who had kept silent for seventeen days, who had pretended not to understand a

word they said, talking to his mother, who was bending an ear to him as if she was hearing his confession. She turned to look over her shoulder, her blue eyes wide with apprehension, this woman who had been not three years older than Frank was now when she crossed the Atlantic ocean alone.

He wants me to take a message, Frank. On the streetcar. Across the town.

The man was a long time writing out his message and giving directions, giving them in English so good it was itself almost a foreign language. The address meant nothing to Frank's mother; she had never been anywhere. Just the same, instead of the shawl she threw over her head to run to Jacobson's grocery in the morning, she put on her Sunday hat. She told Frank to stay in in case their patient would need something, but the man said no; he would be all right and Frank should go with his mother. He told her to take the trolley, that if there was money enough in the house for it, she would have it back before the end of the day. So she took down the box for the second time that morning and took out some coins.

Traffic was a free-for-all of pedestrians and horse-drawn drays and traps, cabs and carriages, bicycles, trolley cars and automobiles sputtering and backfiring and scaring the horses. The trolleys ran three abreast down the middle of the street, but the rest of the traffic never stopped so you could get out to them. As a newsboy Frank had a badge that allowed him to jump on and off the streetcars whenever he wanted, but his mother had never ridden one before and he saw that she never would have if he hadn't come with her; if he hadn't taken hold of her arm, she would have kept running back to the kerb.

They had to change cars twice; the South End and Back Bay might be next-door neighbors, but there was no direct communication between them. They were to tell the driver of the third car they wanted to get to Commonwealth and Hereford. Frank's mother had been practicing saying it under her breath from the moment they started down the steps, Commonwealth and Hereford, please. Commonwealth and Hereford. So when he saw the kind of house they had to approach, two shining doors, each with a bright brass lion head

in the center, Frank was sure her nerve would fail her. But she took him by the hand, as if he were a child, as if it were she who was there to protect him and not the other way around, and walked calmly up the steps.

The grave-faced man who lived in the house started to shut the door as soon as he saw who it was. But Frank's mother was ready with her letter. He took it from her and shut the door, then after a minute opened it again and stared at them. They were to wait inside, he said, as if he couldn't believe it, and they stepped into a hall with a shining floor and wooden walls covered with dark paintings in wide gold frames. A bronze lamp the size of their kitchen hung from the ceiling. One of the doors off the hall was open and they saw into a room as wide as Commonwealth Avenue itself, with windows and wine-colored drapes that went the distance from ceiling to floor. There was furniture enough for five flats, but not a soul to be seen. Frank pointed to a statue the size of a man and told his mother to look, but she shushed him, as if he'd spoken out loud in church. Then a door opened at the end of the hall and a younger man in a black coat with flapping tails walked briskly toward them. Frank had thought the man who opened the door to them was the owner of the house, but now he wasn't so sure.

The younger man's eyes flew from them to the open door and back again, as if worried they might have stolen something while they'd been left standing there. He said it would be a few minutes before Mr. Samuel's things could be got ready and they would be more comfortable waiting downstairs. This man, too, looked at them as if he couldn't believe his eyes. But Frank and his mother were looking at each other. Mr. Samuel? Was that the name of their tramp? He had signed his note SEW, which had puzzled them enough.

They followed the man down a long flight of steps into a basement kitchen where a fat old woman and two thin girls not much older than Frank were working at a long table stirring and mixing and pouring things. Other people, both men and women and all of them wearing aprons or uniforms and shouting orders at each other, were running in and out of the doors off the kitchen, carrying trays and candlesticks and white cloths. Mrs. O'Grady would see they were fed, said the man

in the black coat before dashing back up the steps. The cook set down the bowl she'd been holding in the crook of her arm and looked daggers at the space he'd disappeared from.

They wanted nothing, Frank's mother said. They were not beggars. They had come to deliver a message and had been told to wait in the kitchen. But they would wait outside instead.

They would not. The fat woman spoke with determination, wiping her hands on her apron. They would take a cup of tea. And that one there, she nodded at Frank, would find room for a slice of raisin tart.

They wanted nothing, his mother repeated. Anyone could see the woman had her two hands full.

Ah she did, she did that, but the kettle was always on and it was little enough trouble to wet the tea, and all while she got the tea and cups and cut a wide wedge of tart for Frank, she talked. She had twenty people to cook for that night in honor of Mrs. Fannie Eliot's niece on a visit from Philadelphia. There would be two quarts of creamed oysters, three quarts of hot consomme, seven pounds of codfish in tartar sauce, twenty cups of sweetbreads, five chickens, five pounds of string beans, a ten-pound fillet of beef, five pounds of brussel sprouts, five pounds of mushrooms, five ducks. Lettuce, celery, cheese, olives, biscuits, rolls, ices, tarts, puddings; more food than had passed through Frank's kitchen in his twelve years.

It was never all that food for one meal?! Frank's mother glanced at him quickly, the way she did when she was afraid he might have heard some piece of scandal one of the neighbor women were always bringing in.

It was, said Mrs. O'Grady with immense satisfaction. And she'd the lunch to cook as well, and no one to help her but these two half-witted girls without an ounce of brain between them. Both girls gave great shy smiles, as if they'd been deeply complimented.

It was a shame the young master had not got back from his travels abroad. The old cook smiled, as if she didn't really think it was a shame at all. She knew for a fact that it was not the city of Boston Mrs. Fanny Eliot's niece from Philadelphia was coming to see. Mr. Samuel had promised his mother he'd be back well in time, but they'd had not one

word from him this past three months.

Again, Frank and his mother looked at each other.

The man in black came running down the steps again, in a hat now and gloves, carrying a big soft traveling bag and rugs folded over his arm. He indicated with a flick of his hand that they were to come along and be quick about it. They followed him through a door that led up some steps to the sidewalk half a block away from the front door of the house. A carriage was waiting, the horses pawing the cobbles and tossing their heads. The man in black helped Frank and his mother inside and laid the traveling bag on the seat opposite, with the rugs piled next to them. He shut the door on them and climbed up with the driver.

Frank looked at his mother from time to time, but she was deep inside herself and not a word was spoken all the way back. The direct route was much shorter than the one by trolley, but the drive over the cobbled streets nearly jolted the teeth out of Frank's head, and seemed twice as long as his journey to Commonwealth and Hereford. Up until that morning he had thought of his family's flat, their kitchen, as the center of the universe.

But now he knew they didn't live at the center of anything, that they were on the fringe, hanging onto the edge, camping at the back door of the country, and each clip-clop of the horses' hooves carried them farther away from where life was supposed to be lived.

The black carriage, highly varnished and drawn by a handsome pair of greys, so much finer than the one-horse trap the landlord arrived in on collection days, caused no small commotion when the driver, after shouting down twice to Frank for directions, finally stopped in front of their building. Up and down both sides of the narrow street women and children came swarming out to see what was up, and when they saw it was Mary Ellen Colleran and Frank getting out of that carriage they couldn't decide whether they were more astonished or disappointed. Helping his mother down, Frank had a moment of pride. But the feeling didn't last long; almost immediately, it turned into its opposite. The garbage in the street, the rotten smells, the neglected houses pressed together shoulder-to-shoulder like drunks lined up at a bar, slop pails parked on the steps, mops propped in the doorways. Old

25

Katie Reddington sitting on her front steps smoking her pipe in the sun. Jack Roe's mother combing her hair right there on the sidewalk. Frank's own brother standing there with his mouth hanging open like a moron.

Frank could have stayed down in the street and satisfied the neighbors' curiosity, told where he had been and all he had seen, enjoyed a moment of celebrity. Instead he followed the man in black, who followed his mother up to their flat. But it was even worse inside. The dark stairway and broken steps, the smell of damp, the smell from the privy, the smell of coal and of cabbage. All registered on him for the first time, and for the first time he was ashamed of where he lived.

He waited with his mother in the front room and all the while they waited they stood silently in the window looking down at the carriage in front of their door, the driver snapping his whip at the swarms of boys, Owen among them, who were trying to climb onto it. The neighbor women kept to the sidewalk, gathered in small clusters, gossiping, speculating, glad of the distraction. Frank and his mother were safe from them only as long as the carriage guarded the door, as long as the distinguished stranger in black was with them. The minute they left, there would begin a parade up and down the steps that wouldn't end until every ear on the street had had its fill.

Lying in bed in the kitchen, the man Frank now had to think of as Mr. Samuel had gradually been looking more and more alive. But standing in the sunlight that penetrated the front room, dressed in grey, he looked more than ever like a dying man. The other man must have shaved him, because he couldn't have done it himself without cutting his throat, the way his hand shook as he reached out to the back of a chair to steady himself. Stripped of its beard his face was years younger, but long and naked, his skin the color of a pail of milk. And thin. They could see just how much weight he had lost by the way the clothes hung off him. He could hardly stand up, let alone walk. Frank's mother went to him to save him having to cross the room.

He must have tried to give her money, Frank couldn't see. His mother stood between them, her back to Frank, but he heard her say she would have the trolley fare back and no more. And then he heard her

say that if she had done something, he couldn't hear what, then that was reward enough. Mr. Samuel said nothing else for a long time, only looked at her, then he gave her something, a card. He raised his hand to Frank and said his name to show he knew what it was, then surrendered himself to the man in black, who didn't seem so distinguished after all, who had been standing like a dummy at Mr. Samuel's elbow, hearing nothing, seeing nothing.

Frank was still stationed at the window; his mother went and stood next to him. They saw the women on the sidewalk draw back and clear the way, saw the driver jump down in a hurry, then quickly look up at their building, as if wondering what they had done to his young master in there, as if they might have held him prisoner and starved him half to death. The driver and the man in black practically lifted the invalid into the carriage. His name, Frank now saw from the card his mother held out to him, was Samuel Eliot Walworth, his address the house on Hereford. Satisfied that he was arranged as comfortably as possible, the other two men climbed up to the driver's box, the driver flicked his whip at the air, and the horses began their slow walk home.

Just as the carriage moved forward, the pale face inside the carriage strained forward and looked up at the house. This time Frank, who had not moved quickly enough before, raised a hand. But Mr. Samuel Eliot Walworth, his eyes intent on the window where they were standing, did not seem to see Frank. His mother watched until the carriage was out of sight, then put a hand on his arm. You'll be the happy one, now he's gone, she said.

But Frank knew he would never be happy again.

LET ERIN REMEMBER
The Irish-American influence on traditional music in Ireland

HILARY BRACEFIELD

There is no doubt that Irish traditional music has had a great revival in the last twenty years or so, and with 'Irish' theme pubs springing up all over the globe in the late 1990s, the music to be found within, live or recorded, has put a general seal of approval upon a type of playing that nearly vanished in the early years of the century. Despite the fears of older musicians that the music is not authentic enough and despite worries that it is too commercialised, there is a growing wish among young people to learn and continue their traditions in a way that suits their own age and tastes. Like all traditional music, learnt mainly aurally, Irish music will not stand still, but adapts itself to changing circumstances.

In Ulster there is still plenty of non-commercial traditional music performed in country districts, in family gatherings, pub sessions, and ceilis, and young people are learning to play and sing from their elders. Though this music was probably never at threat, there seems more going on in the 1990s than in the previous twenty years, particularly in Counties Tyrone, Fermanagh, Donegal, Antrim and Armagh. Young people (those under thirty) respect the knowledge and ability of the senior members of the community, but when they discover the influences on older folk, a number of musicians are mentioned who they often assume are deceased neighbours. These musicians include James Morrison, Patrick Sweeney, Paddy Killoran, John McKenna and Hugh Gillespie, but the chief among them is Michael Coleman. I found that virtually none of the young musicians I have worked with had an idea who these men were. Thus the direct knowledge of a vital Irish-American link is dying out; but its importance should not be

allowed to disappear.

A major irony of the revival of Irish traditional music in Ireland in the twentieth century is that it was largely sparked off by recordings of Irish musicians not in their homeland, but in the United States of America, at a time (the 1920s and 1930s) when these musicians would not have dreamed of being recorded at home. Irish emigration to America began largely after peace was established in Europe at the end of the Napoleonic Wars in 1815, when travel became easier and artisans left in search of better conditions. It increased dramatically after the potato famine crisis of 1845, and after that a steady stream of immigrants arrived to build and work in the cities and on the developing railroads. The great migration has never completely ended, but the numbers slowed during World War I and in the 1930s, as America itself went through the Depression.

It seems that as soon as the recording industry began, companies realised that there was a thriving market for their products among the various European immigrant communities. As Richard Spottswood says in his introduction to the New World Anthology record of immigrant folk music,

> catalogues from the nineties were already advertising records in Hebrew, Polish, Czech, Spanish and other languages ... Victor, Columbia, Edison and the smaller companies who were trying to make inroads among immigrants hammered away at dealing through industry journals and house organs.[1]

Spottswood points out that at first these recordings were derived from foreign sources, such as Germany, England, Scandinavia and Russia, where large cities had established recording companies, but this was not a possibility for the Irish community. In fact, most of the early records aimed at the Irish market were of the stage-Irish variety, already present in vaudeville.[2] After the outbreak of World War I the supply of masters from abroad dried up, but the demand had been created. While the immigrants had usually been from impoverished rural backgrounds in the Old World and would never have afforded a phonograph and records, in America, as Richard Spottswood indicates, they

were largely city dwellers and could afford the ten or fifteen dollars required for such luxuries. But the imported masters and the stage-Irish records were not like the rough peasant music of home:'The records sold but they didn't answer the need for real folk music.'[3] By the early 1920s, however, as the record companies were providing Race Records for blues, jazz, gospel music and white county music, they also began to produce rural vernacular music for the immigrant communities, providing what Spottswood sees as priceless documents of genres and traditions often virtually extinct today.

31

Thus it was that some of the great traditional Irish musicians who had emigrated to America in the early years of the century found themselves on record in the 1920s and 1930s to satisfy a burgeoning market. Harry Bradshaw, who has extensively researched this field, traces the beginnings of the 'authentic' Irish product to 1916. As he says,

> A change for the better came about in 1916 through the courage and determination of Cork-born emigrant Ellen O'Byrne,who, with her husband, managed the O'Byrne De Witt Irish Gafonola and Victor Shop in New York's Third Avenue. Ellen's belief was that records of Irish music and song made by real Irish performers would sell, if they were made available. Through an arrangement with Columbia, she made records in 1916 with baritone George Potter and accordion and banjo players Eddie Herborn and James Wheeler. These records were eagerly bought and were an immediate success. The Irish traditional music industry was launched.[4]

The musicians did not, of course, emigrate in order to record. Whether they intended to look for non-musical work or not, they found in New York, Boston, Chicago, Detroit, Philadelphia and a number of other cities and towns a thriving Irish music scene providing entertainment in bars, clubs, restaurants and dance-halls and on the vaudeville circuit. As well, there were weddings and social events: a musician could make money beyond his wildest dreams at home. The possibility of recording was but icing on the cake.

The recording industry was helped by improvements in the 1920s. The original acoustic sound reproduction system, as Bradshaw points out, was too crude for many instruments: violinists were driven to try out a rather strange amplified instrument invented by Augustus Stroh,

with a standard fiddle neck but with the normal body replaced by a soundbox and metal horn. Its harsh metallic sound was not liked by the players. The introduction in 1925 of an electrical process invented by Joseph Maxfield greatly improved tone quality all round, and this is immediately evident in recordings using the new system. In addition, musicians had a further opportunity for dissemination of their music with the commencement of radio broadcasting, particularly from 1922 on. There seems to have been a large number of station broadcasting programmes for Irish immigrants: Harry Bradshaw found the newspaper *Irish World* listing 26 stations offering such programmes in the late 1920s. As with all other kinds of music, however, the success of Irish music commercially in America was deeply affected, though not extinguished, by the Depression, with improvements only recommencing in 1936 or so. While the music of the immigrants continued to dominate the recording studios through to the 1950s, the use of commercial groups from Ireland such as the Chieftans and the Clancey Brothers and Tommy Makem at last brought the homegrown product to commercial success in the United States of America.

One effect of this American Irish music industry was not foreseen or particularly intended. This was the bringing home of the American-produced record to Ireland itself. Most emigrants, in fact, never expected to return and many never made even brief visits home to see their families. But enough did, and it was they who first brought these recordings back to Ireland. They were to have a disproportionate effect: there were simply no equivalent recordings of local traditional musicians being made in the 1920s in Ireland itself. To this day, older musicians in Ireland are divided as to whether this effect was for the good or not; younger musicians, however, have little knowledge of the phenomenon, despite new issues of much of the music.

Who were the musicians in these American recordings? A huge number of Irish musicians were obviously working in the USA in the early twentieth century, but a few names dominate the recording industry, presumably because of their particular ability. Head and shoulders above them all stands Michael Coleman, but others who recorded a considerable amount are James Morrison and Paddy Killoran, togeth-

er with Patrick Sweeney, Hugh Gillespie (all fiddle players), John McKenna (flute) and a number of others. Coleman, Morrison and Killoran, the most recorded performers, were all from Co Sligo and musicians and music scholars continue to ponder why this should be so and, indeed, whether this fact imposed the Co Sligo style on Irish music as a whole. It was probably happenstance that these great musicians did all come from one county; a number of scholars point out that in their home villages none of the three was any more gifted than others who did not emigrate, but they simply had the opportunity to record their abilities in the USA. Even so, the praise heaped on Michael Coleman suggests that no matter what his peers in his home area in Knockgrania were like as fiddle players, he was indeed, exceptional.

33

Coleman made his first recordings in 1921, and the knowledge of his music in Ireland was already evident by 1924. Harry Bradshaw notes some of the reactions. Tommy Flynn, a well-known Sligo fiddler told him:

> I heard of Michael Coleman about 1924 and I thought he was wonderful altogether. The first Coleman record I heard was *The Boys at the Lough*. I was only starting at the fiddle then, and to hear him play wasn't good encouragement because he was far ahead of every other one. The records were sent home from America or they were sold in the local towns. Half-a-crown they were in them days. You could buy gramophones in Sligo or in the local towns around. Not every house would have one, but any one that liked music, they were off to hear the gramophone.[6]

John Donahue, a flute player from Co Roscommon, said, 'Coleman's records, ah, let me alone! You wouldn't be tired listening to them', and John Blessing, another flute player from Co Leitrim told Bradshaw, 'When Coleman's records came here, he put the real touch to it. The old players thought he was a genius because no one could take music out of a fiddle like he could.'[7]

Tommy Flynn names Coleman's recording of *The Boys at the Lough* as important to him, and this record, from 1921, has become ever more associated with Coleman's name. Curiously, as Bradshaw notes, this Vocalion record and another with *The Shashkeen Reel* were distributed in Ireland on an English label, Beltona, with Coleman given the

name Dennis Malloy, and he was called Daniel Keller on a Pathé disc of *Wellington's Reels and Dougherty's Jigs* from 1923 reissued on Cameo and Lincoln labels, but as Bradshaw says, 'There was no mistaking Coleman's unique sound and jaunty style, or his individual way of addressing a tune.'[8]

There is no doubt that the recordings of all the Irish-American artists from 1921 onwards, well into the 1940s (Michael Coleman died in 1945, James Morrison in 1947 and Paddy Killoran in 1965) had a galvanising effect on the development of Irish traditional music in Ireland itself, but the haphazard nature of its dissemination was countered only by the founding of the organisation *Chomhaltas Ceoltóirí Eireann* in 1951, which seeks to promote the traditional music, song and dance of Ireland, and to preserve the traditions wherever possible. The foundation of Irish Broadcasting in 1926 was another milestone, with its director, Seamus Clandillon, sympathetic to the broadcasting of traditional music, but again it was the 1950s before there was regular broadcasting of local musicians. The developing pride in the home grown product led to some condemnation by scholars of the influence of the Irish-American performers which has not yet completely dissipated. It seems to have been led by the important musician and scholar Seán Ó Riada (1931-71), a classical composer and traditional fiddle player who combined a career in classical music (working for Radio Eireann, the Abbey Theatre and University College, Cork) with the leadership of a traditional music group, *Ceoltóirí Chualann.* In a series of radio talks, *Our Musical Heritage* in 1962, published in 1982, he spoke of Michael Coleman in a way that is often echoed even today:

> Undoubtedly, the strongest influence on fiddle-players so far was that brilliant virtuoso of traditional fiddle-music, the late Michael Coleman. Coleman was from Sligo, but while his style stems from the Sligo style, it developed into something all his own. The tragedy is that so many fiddle players nowadays are imitating that highly personal style of his instead of developing the styles of their own areas to suit themselves. An imitation is only an imitation, no matter how good it is, a sign that the player lacks imagination, a confession of failure.[9]

The influence of the Irish-American recordings by both fiddlers and

other musicians on older players in the south of Ireland is reasonably well documented. The influence also extends into Ulster. Undergraduate students in the Music Department of the University of Ulster write a final-year dissertation and many choose to write about Irish traditional music. These students are usually players or singers in the field, and when they interview older musicians the names of the Irish-American performers are often cited as influences, with the uninitiated student at first usually assuming that they are other contemporary local players. It appears that virtually none of these young players previously knew of the Irish-American recording connection, so the worries of scholars that it might perpetually adversely affect local traditions are probably unfounded.

I will discuss just seven of the dissertations in each of which the student had to research the Irish-American connection once she had interviewed her chosen musicians. Only a few dissertations so far have investigated traditional music in Co Antrim, but in 1989 Fionnuala O'Connell worked on fiddle playing in parts of the county. The isolation of the county has perhaps helped its players retain their individual styles, and, if anything, the five players interviewed by Fionnuala acknowledge that their main influences were Scottish styles of fiddling. But Dennis Sweeney from Randalstown said that 'he played reels and jigs in the Sligo style, being influenced by those famous players, Michael Coleman and Paddy Killoran',[10] and John McKillop from Carnlough travelled widely in Canada and America and feels that not only was he influenced by Michael Coleman and James Morrison, but also by the Scottish fiddler Scott Skinner and by blues, jazz and French-Canadian music. One of the tunes that he has made his own is a version of *The Tennessee Waltz*.[11]

Co Donegal is also isolated, and again recognises in its players the close relationships with Scottish traditional music. Nicola Scott in her dissertation *Fiddling in County Donegal* (1993) notes some influence of the commercial recordings of Michael Coleman on the Donegal fiddlers, but in her interviews with present-day musicians found that they acknowledged mainly the contribution of the Donegal Doherty family and of Scottish music, even though often adapted into a Donegal

35

style. None of the three master fiddlers she interviewed, Danny O'Donnell of the Rosses, Con Cassidy (Teelin) and Vincent Campbell (Glenties) specifically mentioned Irish-American players, not even Hugh Gillespie, who was a pupil and friend of Michael Coleman, and who came from Co Donegal. In fact, Danny O'Donnell, speaking in 1979 to the authors of the important collection *The Northern Fiddler: Music and Musicians of Donegal and Tyrone* shows both some knowledge and some insularity when discussing the lilting tradition:

> It was the women mostly who do the lilting. I remember hearing Michael Coleman playing *Miss McCloud's Reel* for the first time. I had heard it lilted since I was a child and was amazed to hear the exact tune he played was in the lilting of the women. Now we had no connection with Sligo at all, so I gathered from that that the lilting must have been a very old widespread practice.[12]

It seems that in Co Donegal the traditions of local districts were so strong and so isolated even from each other that the Irish-American records had very little impact. The travelling of labourers to and from Scotland, however, kept up a tradition of mutual respect and influence. Yet there was still some knowledge of the recordings.

The ceili band produces a sound that typifies 'Irish music' to many people outside Ireland. Enjoyment of ceilis has increased in country districts in recent years, after first the showband and then modern forms of entertainment almost obliterated them in the 1970s and 1980s. Because of the instruments used in a ceili band one can see the influence of the Irish-American recordings. Seán Ó Riada would have us believe that the idea emanated in Ireland:

> In 1926, Seamus Clandillon, the first Director of Irish Broadcasting, conceived the idea of the céilí band: eight or nine musicians playing together. One of the most successful of the early groups was the old Ballinakill Céilí Band, which consisted of two fiddles, two flutes, and two accordions, with neither drums, piano nor double-bass.[13]

But Ó Riada goes on to deride recent bands who use not only piano, drums and double-bass, but even saxophones, guitar and banjo, in an oblique way. Ó Riada is decrying the sound of the Irish groups of the

American recordings. Elsewhere in his talks he has condemned the piano accompaniment used by Michael Coleman for most of his recordings:

> The traditional fiddle-player who insists on a piano accompaniment is falling into {a} trap of 'respectability.' ...The tragedy is that the people in charge of recording Coleman were ignorant enough to think he needed a piano accompaniment.[14]

Linda Heaney in her dissertation on the John Murphy Ceili Band from Armagh(1995), traces the ceili back to the house ceilis of the eighteenth and nineteenth centuries where stories were told and recitations given as well as singing and dancing and the playing of instruments. Sometimes, she was told by Sean O'Driscoll of the John Murphy Ceili Band, house ceilis were prearranged to mark a special occasion such as the harvest, visitors from America, or before emigrations: these were known as 'American wakes'. These were all winter ceilis: in the summer they were held at cross-roads or on a 'moinin' (a green grassy patch). It was in the mid-twentieth century that the clergy, often opposed to the drinking and promiscuity of the cross-road ceilis, realised their popularity and possible source of income and began welcoming ceilis into parochial halls.[15]

The members of the John Murphy Ceili Band to whom Linda spoke acknowledged the influence of the broadcasts of the Ballinakill Ceili Band, and of ceili bands from Scotland such as Timmy Shannon's and Tommy McCloud's, popular in the 1930s and 1940s. But far more, Linda found, the members of all the earlier Ulster bands in Co Armagh were influenced by the music of the Irish-American recording artists. The John Murphy Ceili Band was formed in 1956 and had huge popularity, through live performances throughout Ireland and broadcasts on both BBC Radio Ulster and Radio Eireann into the 1990s, though personnel have come and gone. Linda interviewed John Murphy himself, the leader and fiddle player, and also Sean O'Driscoll (piano) and Dennis Heaney (accordion). All stressed the importance of the American records.

John Murphy was born in 1926 outside Crossmaglen in Co Armagh.

His mother played fiddle and his father fiddle and concertina. John told Linda that his father

> had a great interest in traditional music. He was especially interested in Irish-American players. Some of John's earliest memories were of his father's gramophone and the collection of records he had. As Pat Murphy was predominantly a fiddle player he had an extensive collection of recordings by fiddle players such as Michael Coleman, Paddy Killoran and Hugh Gillespie.[16]

Linda found that her sources particularly praised the fiddle playing of Michael Coleman as a great inspiration. Hugh Gillespie (from Co Donegal) is important because as well as his association with Coleman, beginning when he emigrated in 1928, he worked with groups and bands, especially the Star of Erin Orchestra and the Four Provinces Orchestra, returning to Ballybofey, Co Donegal in 1977 and dying in 1995. To members of the ceili band, however, the recordings of Paddy Killoran and his Pride of Erin Orchestra were particularly important. John Murphy stated that Paddy Killoran's band 'was one of the biggest influences on the development of ceili bands in Ireland in the twentieth century'.[17] The band included Killoran and Patrick Sweeney (violins), with piano, accordion and banjo. It seems that the use of the piano and of certain other instruments so derided by Ó Riada, became well-established: John Murphy's own initial line-up included three fiddles, piano, mandolin, guitar and drums, and accordion was soon added. Sean O'Driscoll does say, however, that though he always played piano in broadcasts, he did not usually attend ceilis, partly because of his work responsibilities, partly because 'not every hall had a piano, [and in those which had] most were not fit to play'.[18]

We come now to Co Tyrone, which appears to have a particularly thriving tradition to this day, and which, of all the northern counties, has been particularly influenced by the Irish-American recordings. Feldman and O'Doherty actually stated in 1979 , 'The vast majority of Tyrone fiddlers who are currently active possess a repertoire and play in a style that is derived from the recorded fiddling of the Sligo artist Michael Coleman and from the ceildh [sic] bands that have been pop-

ular there since the 1940s.' They go on to say that in their interviews with Tyrone fiddlers there were three kinds of responses: some stopped playing in public altogether, some used them as a source of new tunes, but others replayed the records 'till they could imitate Coleman's playing note for note. Such was the combined power of Coleman's virtuosity and of the new technology of recording on the isolated musical culture of Tyrone'.[19] Feldman and O'Doherty think that the Tyrone fiddlers rejected their own local repertoire and playing characteristics entirely, but this was debatable even in 1979, and is not true today.

39

Claire McMullen in 1996 compared the music of two Co Tyrone ceili bands. Because she was enquiring about the nature of the bands' work, and of the dances and format of the Co Tyrone ceili, she did not enquire deeply into the origins of the style. It is interesting to note that the older band whose music she studied, formed by the late Francis Murphy of Fivemiletown in the early 1950s, was called the Pride of Erin Ceili Band, surely a homage to Paddy Killoran's band. She did interview the fiddle player Felix Kearney of Omagh, one of the band's most famous members, but he only admitted to the influence of a well-known older local fiddler, Jimmy Carson. The student did not, however, gather any information which could confirm an American influence. She compared this older band with a much younger group, the Emerald Ceili Band, started in 1989 by Gerald and Paul Morgan, aged 13 and 15. This band has been most successful, featuring on radio and television as well as in live playing. Claire noticed differences between the bands. The Pride of Erin had a larger line-up (three fiddles, two flutes, two accordions, piano and drums, as against fiddle, flute, banjo, accordion, keyboard and drums), and played with more ornamentation and more variations. Most obvious, though, is that the younger group betrays an influence of show-band and country and western music, and play in general much faster. Thus new elements are entering traditional music and the older influences are fading.

Two dissertations studied fiddle playing in the county: Deirdre Walsh's in 1991 on the Kearney family, and Shona Cunningham in 1996 on a number of players, including the Kearney brothers. This family was not studied in detail by Feldman and O'Doherty, but are very influential players and teachers. Felix Kearney junior (b.1913) has been mentioned above as a member of the Pride of Erin Ceili Band. Both Deirdre and Shona interviewed him as well, and although he mentioned the influence of the local fiddler Jim Carson, he is loathe to acknowledge influences from America. But Deirdre elicited from him an influence of Jack and Pat Gallagher. Jack Gallagher spent most of his working life in America and played with Michael Coleman, James Morrison and Paddy Killoran. Deirdre notes that Pat Gallagher, his son, 'learnt his techniques from his father and went on to copy extensively the Coleman style of playing'. But she also records a story that when Felix was about fifteen, his father (also a famous musician) heard him practising two new tunes he had learned from Pat Gallagher. On being told Felix was trying to copy the style, his father replied, 'If you haven't a style of your own, you'll never be a fiddler.'[20] It is perhaps because of this that Felix Kearney does not wish to acknowledge influences. His brother, Arthur (b.1921) was also unwilling to reveal American influences, but did mention to Shona that he thought that 'the Tyrone style would have been based on Michael Coleman for a time. Then it changed to become more soft with well-defined ornamentation'.[21] A year later, in 1997, however, Arthur talked to Grainne Warnock, who was comparing the styles of Counties Tyrone and Clare, and he expanded on the topic:

> As far as recordings were concerned, Arthur said that it was not until he was about fifteen that he heard Michael Coleman. 'Then again,' he said, 'not everyone had a gramophone.' Arthur believed that Coleman was a great boost to him and music in general throughout Ireland … Coleman was, though, beyond the capabilities of most Irish musicians at this time.[22]

Francie Quinn, a fiddle player in his late sixties, told Shona quite proudly of the influence of the recordings of Coleman's music, and she also talked to Mickey Gallagher, brother of Pat Gallagher, now deceased, but mentioned above by Felix Kearney. He, too, recognised that the Tyrone style has perhaps been over-influenced from outside, but thought that young players were developing it again. It 'had

become very elaborate and fast, but perhaps too fast', he said, rather disapprovingly.[22] Both he and Arthur Kearney were sorry that the slow air seemed to be disappearing; on the other hand some of the students from Co Tyrone writing on vocal music have found it to be thriving in that form.

41

It is curious that all the older Tyrone fiddlers are defensive about the influence of Michael Coleman, Pat Gallagher and the Irish-American musicians. Both Arthur Kearney and Tommy John Quinn, an accordion player, when interviewed by Grainne felt that there was not a distinctive Tyrone style, mainly because of the effect of Coleman and the others. Despite this, however, all the students found distinctive personal styles in the players they studied and differences from players from other areas. And those who studied younger players, such as Claire McMullan (the Emerald Ceili Band) and Grainne Warnock (a number of younger players) noted new styles entering the arena – often spoken of half-disapprovingly by the older players. They all seem to play too fast! It is evident in what the students found and from what they know themselves that direct knowledge of the Irish-American connection has largely disappeared. It is now filtered through the playing styles of those older folk who heard the music in the periods 1920–1940 on their gramophones, but who absorbed it into their own personal way of playing. But through their acknowledgment, and through recent releases on cassette and CD of much of the repertoire, the importance of this Irish-American connection will always form a significant part in the development of Irish traditional music in Ireland and in the wider world.

ENDNOTES

42

1 Sleevenotes by Richard Spottswood, 'Folk Music of Immigrants from Europe and the Near East', *Old Country Music in a New Land*, introductory essay, New World Anthology of Music, NW264, 1977.

2 See Harry Bradshaw, *Michael Coleman 1891-1945*, (Dublin: *Viva Voce*, 1991), p.52.

3 Spottswood, op. cit.

4 Bradshaw, p.52.

5 Bradshaw, pp.55-56.

6 Bradshaw, pp.58-59.

7 Bradshaw, pp.58-59.

8 Bradshaw, pp.58-59.

9 Seán Ó Riada, *Our Musical Heritage*, (Portlaoise, The Dolmen Press, 1982), p.53.

10 Fionnuala O'Connell, *Traditional Fiddle-playing in County Antrim: Its Origins and Characterisics* (unpublished dissertation, University of Ulster, 1989), p.24.

11 O'Connell, p.38.

12 Allen Feldman and Eamonn O'Doherty, *The Northern Fiddler: Music and Musicians of Donegal and Tyrone* (Belfast, Blackstaff Press, 1979), p.148.

13 Ó Riada, p.73.

14 Ó Riada, p.59.

15 Linda Heaney, *The John Murphy Ceili Band* (unpublished dissertation, University of Ulster, 1995), ch.1, pp.3–5.

16 Heaney, ch.3, p.1.

17 Heaney, ch.2, pp.1–2.

18 Heaney, ch.3, p.7.

19 Feldman and O'Doherty, p.197.

20 Deirdre Walsh, *Traditional Irish Music and the Kearney Family's Ongoing Contribution in Tyrone* (unpublished dissertation, University of Ulster, 1991), p.37.

21 Shona Cunningham, *The Tradition of Fiddle Playing in Co Tyrone* (unpublished dissertation,University of Ulster, 1996), p.17.

22 Grainne Warnock, *A Comparison of Traditional Music in Co Tyrone with that of Co Clare* (unpublished dissertation, University of Ulster, 1997), p.7.

23 Cunningham, p.15.

The author gratefully acknowleges the work of all her undergraduate dissertion students in Irish traditional music, particularly Fionnuala O'Connell, Nicola Scott, Linda Heaney, Claire McMullan, Deirdre Walsh, Shona Cunningham and Grainne Warnock, and the assistance of the Irish Traditional Music Archive, 63 Merrion Square, Dublin.

DAVY CROCKETT
The Man and the Legend

MATT McKEE

In 1889 an organisation was founded which deliberately promoted the idea that regionally, racially and culturally, America (particularly Appalachian America) and Ulster were linked by strong historic ties. Calling itself the Scotch-Irish Society of America, it was founded on the premise that there was a unique 'race' and culture which could be classified as distinctly Scotch-Irish. This was not, as the name might imply, a racial mixture of Scots and Irish people. Rather, it was a geographic definition used to signify that the Scotch-Irish of America had come to the New World from Scotland via Ulster. In order to promote the achievements of the 'race', the Society typically adopted the following technique. It selected prominent American public figures and claimed on their behalf a Scotch-Irish heritage. Often the links between such figures and the Scotch-Irish 'race' were extremely tenuous. Abraham Lincoln, for example, was claimed merely on the grounds that he was born in Kentucky, had a supposedly Scotch-Irish name, and could '... love as tenderly as an Irishman and hold by principle with the tenacity of a Scotsman'.[1] This convention is still used today by similar societies and individuals who are now more commonly known as Ulster-Scots.

Perhaps one of the most colourful figures so selected was the legendary Davy Crockett. Davy was an obvious choice, a ready-made, American hero whose reputation by the mid-nineteenth century had already achieved mythical proportions. Stripped of their romantic gloss, however, the facts about Davy's life, though commendable, are less colourful than the fiction which came to surround them. He was born in 1786 on the American frontier in what is now Greene County,

east Tennessee. During the War of 1812–14 he served variously as a volunteer mounted rifleman, Indian spy, and battalion commander. Entering local politics, he was twice elected to the Tennessee legislature. At a national level, he was also elected three times to the United States Congress. Following his defeat in the 1835 congressional election, he abandoned both politics and Tennessee and left for Texas where he died a year later at the Alamo. Summing up his life, the inscription on his headstone reads: 'Davy Crockett, Pioneer, Patriot, Soldier, Trapper, Explorer, State Legislator, Congressman, Martyred at The Alamo. 1786–1836'.

Underlying these achievements was a forceful personality shaped by a violent and unstable frontier environment. Davy's grandparents, for example, having newly settled in East Tennessee from North Carolina were killed by Creek and Cherokee Indians in 1777 while his father and uncles were serving with the Revolutionary Army. This was nine years before Davy was born, but during his own lifetime he himself continually experienced violence and upheaval. While living in a log-cabin tavern run by his father, the twelve-year-old Davy got into a fight on his first and only week at school and ran away from home to avoid punishment. Demonstrating his self-reliance, he joined a cattle drive to Virginia where he spent the next two and a half years working for farmers, waggoners, and a hat maker. Returning home at fifteen, his sense of family duty prompted him to work without pay for men to whom his father owed money. During this period he also attended school for six months. Apart from the four days when he was twelve, this was the only formal education he received. Often borrowing his employer's rifle he became an expert shot, a skill which later gained him a distinguished reputation as marksman, hunter and Indian fighter. In a single year he was reported to have killed one hundred and five bears, a feat respected among the large hunting fraternity of Tennessee.

Capitalising on his popularity and military reputation, Davy entered Tennessee politics. Undaunted by his lack of education, he wooed the electorate by his wit and good humour. For example, one of his favourite electioneering ploys was to carry a twist of chewing tobacco and a bottle of liquor. After offering a prospective voter the bottle,

Crockett would hand him a 'chaw' of tobacco to replace the one he had to discard to take the drink. Thus, as Davy reasoned, 'He would not be worse off than when I found him; and I would be sure to leave him in a first-rate good humour.'[2] On several occasions he embarrassed his political opponents by a combination of ridicule and trickery. Once, for example, he memorised an opponent's standard campaign speech and delivered it verbatim just before the other was about to speak. On another occasion, it is reported, while forced to spend the night at an inn with his congressional rival, Adam ('Pegleg') Huntsman, Davy got up in the middle of the night and pretended to force the bed room door of the inn keeper's daughter. As he used a chair to mimic the sound of his rival's wooden leg pounding on the bare floor boards, Huntsman got the blame. However, his opponent had the last laugh when the electorate chose him over Davy for the 1835 congressional election. In a remark which typified his devil-may-care attitude, Davy is supposed to have said: 'Since you have chosen to elect a man with a timber toe to succeed me, you may all go to hell and I will go to Texas.'[3]

Fighting for Texas independence, Davy met a hero's death at the Alamo. Besieged for 11 days awaiting reinforcements which never arrived and fast running out of ammunition, he and 186 companions withstood Santa Anna's 5,000 strong Mexican army. When the smoke of battle cleared, Davy and all his companions lay dead, but so too did over 2,000 Mexicans. Differing accounts arose as to whether Crockett died defending his post to the last in hand-to-hand combat or was forced to surrender and was executed by a firing squad. Either way, his death was suitably heroic.

In the account so far what is there to connect Crockett regionally, racially or culturally with Ulster? He himself seemed either unaware of the fact or completely indifferent to it. Not that this necessarily negates the validity of the claim. Andrew Jackson, who was demonstrably of Scotch-Irish descent displayed a similar attitude. However, for some members of the Scotch-Irish and Ulster-Scot societies the mere fact that Crockett came from Tennessee was evidence enough that he must have had Ulster links. So many early representatives of the Scotch-Irish

'race' had settled in Southern Appalachia during the 18th-century, particularly in Tennessee, argued the Secretary of the Scotch-Irish Society in 1889, that it was '… about the center of the blood in the United States.'[4] Had Pennsylvania been chosen for this honour his assertion might have been more accurate.

It was also argued that there were strong historic connections between the two regions. Like many of his predecessors, a more recent commentator, Billy Kennedy, links the regions with the two great events of Scotch-Irish history, the Williamite Cause in Ireland and the Revolutionary War in America. The former was a struggle for religious freedom, the latter for political independence, and the Scotch-Irish, it has been argued, were predominant in both. Several of Davy's ancestors, Kennedy claims, were involved in the Siege of Londonderry in 1690 and his father and uncles took part in the various Revolutionary War campaigns including the Battle of King's Mountain in 1780.[5]

Racially, it seems, the Crocketts were Scotch-Irish simply by virtue of the fact that they had gone to America from Ulster and the definition had little to do with their actual racial origins. They were, in fact, writes Kennedy, of French extraction and had come to Ulster during the Plantation of James I. So long as they were not Irish, it appears, almost any race who had immigrated to America from Ulster could meet the Scotch-Irish racial criterion. If the term 'Scotch-Irish' is taken as a narrow racial definition based on 'race purity', whatever that might be, the Crocketts would have been disqualified. However, in the broader sense, which implies an identity based on a more regional and cultural definition, their sojourn in Ulster fully entitled them to the title.

More difficult to defend is the assertion that certain inherited racial characteristics were uniquely Scotch-Irish and had been passed on to Davy. It argued that these had been forged in the frontier conditions in both Ulster and America and had made the 'race' the most successful of the pioneers.[6] 'Those who conquered Transappalachia,' comments A.K. Moore, 'were demonstrably filled with bright visions of racial destiny and with a strong spirit of aggression.' He suggests that two main reasons were responsible for their success. 'Desire for the promised land,' he argues, 'actualizes as concerted movement only when the

48

energy level is high throughout a people.' In addition, there was a strong psychological factor. 'Obstacles pose a challenge,' he asserts, 'and evoke in warlike men a blind passion to conquer. ... Moreover, the backwoodsmen were denied the wonderful garden land by the royal Proclamation of 1763 and by the opposition of the Indians, both of which deterrents probably had the psychological effect of provoking them.'[7]

49

Although Moore refers to immigrants from the British Isles general-ly, the Scotch-Irish argued that they had been the leading 'race' in the conquest of Transappalachia and, therefore, these racial attributes and achievements belonged exclusively to them. Both accounts conve-niently ignore the racial dynamism which, it could be equally argued, had motivated other races, notably the Spanish and French. However this may be, Davy, it was claimed, possessed these racial traits to an unusually high degree. Had he not throughout his life, for example, demonstrated 'energy' and the 'spirit of aggression' both as frontiers-man surrounded by hostile wilderness and hidden enemies, and, most notably, as one of the defenders of Texas independence faced by impos-sible odds at the Alamo? So far as his self-reliance and obligation to family were concerned, although admirable qualities, neither were exclusively Scotch-Irish racial characteristics. Even less so, perhaps, was his famous good-natured humour, which was a trait more associated with the jovial 'pure' Irish than the dour 'Scotch' Irish.

Culturally, Crockett's connections with Ulster were equally indeter-minate. The most important aspect of Scotch-Irish culture was Presbyterianism, out of which, it was argued, had arisen a love of edu-cation and a passion for the principle of political democracy. Davy was neither noticeably religious nor well educated. However, he was an astute politician. Even though the political success of the Scotch-Irish is greatly exaggerated, it is perhaps no accident that from Jackson to Woodrow Wilson ten of the twenty Presidents of the United States were demonstrably of Scotch-Irish descent and may have owed some-thing to their cultural heritage. Apparently benefiting by this acclaimed inheritance, Davy had gone far in his political career. Although he failed to achieve the success of his contemporary, Andrew Jackson, it

might be argued that he was more committed to the democratic process and was more closely representative of the 'common man' than Jackson himself. For example, he opposed Jackson by proposing a bill to make Tennessee public land freely available to poor squatters, a measure which would have enfranchised greater numbers. As Michael A. Lofara, one of Davy's biographers, remarks: 'His humor and, somewhat ironically, his lack of extraordinary success and achievement, may well have kept Crockett a more attainable and attractive ideal in the popular mind during his public career.'[8]

This is not to suggest that the memory of Davy Crockett ever faded from the popular mind. Almost immediately with the death of the man was born the legend. Indeed, it can be argued that the process had begun earlier and Davy himself was partly responsible. As raconteur, for example, he inserted himself into the folk stories he related. Following the normal manner of myth-building, the legend was then perpetuated through an oral tradition where stories featuring Davy were related by others. Additionally, a literary genre emerged in which a separate body of legends were attributed to him. In the play *The Lion of the West* (1830), Nymrod Wildfire was a stage representation of Davy. Again, the actor Frank Mayo enjoyed great success as co-author and leading man in *Davy Crockett: Or, Be Sure You're Right Then Go Ahead.*

Contributing to the literary tradition himself, Davy collaborated with the authors of two biographies of his life and deeds. In 1833 *The Life and Adventures of Colonel David Crockett of West Tennessee* was published, and two years later, in a bid to drum up support for a proposed presidential campaign, the Whigs produced an account of his travels in the North and East. Some of the stories contained in these accounts were reprinted in a series of popular Crockett Almanacs which were published from 1835 to 1856. More often, however, the stories in the almanacs were pure inventions which had little relationship with any of the original tales. Usually they were spine-chilling narratives of hunts, comic pieces in Dutch (German) dialect, and humorous stories of the frontier. Always, however, the fictional Davy was the hero. Surpassing the exploits of Baron Munchausen, he had an underwater

battle with a giant cat-fish, twisted the tail off Halley's comet, swam up Niagara Falls on an alligator, and unfroze the axels of the earth and sun with hot bear grease. By 1849 his legend had become so popular that an English traveller to America observed that 'everything here is Davy Crockett'. Everyone knew he took hailstones for life pills, picked his teeth with a pitchfork, fanned himself with a hurricane, wore a cast-iron shirt, and drank creosote and aquafortis. He could jump higher, dive deeper and come up dryer than anyone else, and was 'half-horse, half-allegator and a bit of snapping turtle.'[9]

Although slightly less sensational, the legend of Davy Crockett was carried on in the twentieth century through a series of silent and modern films that culminated in the Fess Parker and John Wayne portrayals of Davy. In these he was always the courageous defender of his country and protector of the weak. Whatever the various changes may have been, through a combination of force of personality, self-promotion and imaginative fiction, Crockett became a legend. There emerged, claims Lofora, an attractive mythical figure: 'He is congressman, speculator, superman, blazing patriot, boisterous braggart, and backwoods trickster, but all these roles are smoothly dissolved by a broad, puckish, good humor and recast into a single fun-loving, dominant presence.'[10]

The connection between the mythical Crockett and Ulster is even more superficial than that between the Province and the man, since it, naturally, mythologizes him along American lines, using Southwestern humour and the Tall Tale, both American genres, as the obvious vehicles. Ulster, of course, had a rich oral folklore tradition which, it has been argued, the Scotch-Irish took with them to America and which may have facilitated the reception and influenced the creation of future myths. This tradition survived into the late nineteenth century and beyond. In 1993, for example, a member of the Scotch-Irish Society told how a woman threatened her children with a 'bogeyman' figure from the seventeenth century who had pursued the Scots Covenanters. Therefore, he concluded, the folk memory was long and enduring in Southern Appalachia which demonstrated 'the primitive character of these people and their hold upon their traditions.'[11]

51

Awareness of such folklore is quite plausible; however, how conscious a largely illiterate people were of ancient Ulster legends which were best known in a literary form is more questionable. The much earlier Finn and Cuchulain Cycles, for example, which described the deeds of famous Irish giants and warriors, were best known by Irish-Americans, particularly those concerned with the cause of Irish nationalism and influenced by the Gaelic revival. Any similarity between these legends and the legend of Davy Crockett, therefore, was unlikely to result from the folklore tradition of the Scotch-Irish, but may have been purely coincidental. Arguably, the closest link between the Ulster Cycles and the Scotch-Irish was in the actual collection and publication of the tales themselves, as many of those responsible were Ulster-Scot Presbyterians.

Unavoidably, perhaps, there were some similarities between the legends in setting and content. Both were located in wild and rugged regions where game was plentiful and danger and violence never far away. Both contained accounts of daring deeds, tall tales, and humorous anecdotes, all of which influenced their subsequent respective oral traditions and national literatures. In addition, the heroes were stoical, chivalrous, and virtually indestructible. Davy and Cuchulain, for example, were both typical of the superman hero. Just as Davy, the Lion of the West, had 'killed him a bear when he was only three', as the ballad in the Walt Disney film of 1955 tells us, Cuchulain, the Hound of Ulster, had similarly throttled a giant guard dog at an equally tender age. Just as Davy was an expert marksman with his rifle, so was Cuchulain with his spear. However, such similarities between the Crockett myth and the Ulster tradition were not unique and may be found in many other ancient legends. Indeed, it seems to be a universal prerequisite among all cultures that their legendary heroes must possess super-human courage, strength and skill.

The differences between the two legends are perhaps more marked than the similarities. The Ulster Cycles were set in a provincial, hierarchical society, and were full of archaic mysticism, superstition, and supernatural events. The Crockett legend, on the other hand, was national, democratic, modern, and light-hearted in tone. Much of

Davy's comedy, for example, was derived from dialect stories featuring German settlers in Southern Appalachia. It is argued that this is a peculiarly American phenomenon because of the numerous immigrant groups within the dominant English-speaking culture and demonstrates the cosmopolitan nature of American society. Davy, the legendary hero as well as the man, also stood as a figure of political and social democracy. He was chosen as a folk hero not because he was unique, but because he was representative of his fellow citizens. Although Davy was always the central figure, the tales portrayed the common frontiersman in his daily pursuits and revealed him as a distinct generic type in speech, manners, and dress. Although regional in character, he was also recognisably uniquely American. Davy was a republican, an individual, paid homage to no one, made up his own mind, and was full of tenacity and self-confidence. His attitude to life was summed up in his simple motto, 'Be sure you're right and go ahead'.

Neither the legend of Davy Crockett nor the man, it must be admitted, have much direct connection with Ulster. He was an American, after all, who operated exclusively within an American political and social framework. However, in the absence of more concrete evidence, there are those who employ stories, beliefs, behaviours, speech patterns, songs, and whatever else they can find, as proof that Appalachia's culture can be traced back to Northern Ireland. This method may be quite legitimate when it comes to general assumptions concerning the possible antecedents of large groups and their common culture. Unfortunately, when it comes to specific assertions about individuals it is somewhat less reliable. Applying such a liberal methodology, as we have seen with Abraham Lincoln, almost anyone from Southern Appalachia can be linked to Ulster. In the case of Davy Crockett, the connections are firmer, but still only based on a rather loose historical and regional foundation. There is little substantial evidence that racially or culturally he owed anything to a Scotch-Irish inheritance. The only real links are that Davy's ancestors had come from Ulster to America and that he was born in a region which contained a large proportion of people who shared a similar background.

53

Enchanted Mesas
2nd panel of triptych, bichromate print
KEN DIXON
TEXAS TECH UNIVERSITY

ENDNOTES

1   Dr. D.C. Kelley, 'Minutes and Short Addresses (morning session)', *Proceedings of the Scotch-Irish Congress* (published by order of the Scotch-Irish Society of America, Robert Clarke and Co. 1889, 10 volumes. 1889–1896, 1900–1901), Vol.1, p.55.

2   Michael A. Lofaro 'From David to Davy: The Growth of the Legendary Crockett', in Robert J. Higgs, Ambrose N. Manning, and Jim Wayne Miller, *Appalacia Inside Out*: Volume 1 Conflict and Change, University of Tennessee Press, Knoxville, 1995, p.53.

3   Ibid., p.54.

4   A. C. Floyd, 'Objects and Results', in *Proceedings*, v.1, p.5. See also John Allison, "Scotch-Irish Founders of the Volunteer State", in ibid., Vol.9, p.151.

5   Billy Kennedy, *The Scots-Irish in the Hills of Tennessee*, Causeway Press, Londonderry, 1995, pp.99–109.

6   H. Tyler Blethen, 'The Scotch-Irish Heritage of Southern Appalachia', in Higgs et al, *Appalachia Inside Out*, p.4.

7   Arthur K. Moore, *The Frontier Mind*, University of Kentucky Press, London, 1963, pp. 47–8.

8   Lofara, in Higgs et al., *Appalachia Inside Out*, p.54.

9   Captain R.G.A. Levinge, in Richard M. Dorson, *America in Legend: Folklore from the Colonial Period to the Present*, Random House, New York, 1973, pp.76–7.

10 Lofara, in Higgs et al., *Appalachia Inside Out*, pp.56–7.

11 Colonel William Preston Johnson, 'The Scotch-Irish of Western Virginia', *Proceedings*,Vol 5, p.200.

Before You
linocut
DAVID DUBOSE
SEACOURT WORKSHOP

VETERANS, ANTRIM COAST 1994

FRANK ORMSBY

The veterans arrived at sundown and parked their car
by the perimeter fence. Or where the fence had been.
Now there were fields, an established willow-grove,
a dirt-track, half-covered, that was after their time.
    They liked that soft forgetfulness, the slow
effacement of green places starting again each spring.

Later, they walked the town and were content
    to ask directions, stroll as casual ghosts
that knew what they knew and nobody recognized.
Here, too, the years receded. They liked that free fall
    of history settling and had brought no addresses.

They might have lingered there until it was time,
    the precise hour, then taken the coastal road,
        as fifty years before. Instead they chose
    to ponder the spring moon, to gaze in a field
while Normandy waited. The moonlight poured down
on the immense, earned accomplishment of their veteran calm.

MOLLY AND CLYDE

DOUGLAS CARSON

What follows is a chapter from a forthcoming book – *The Titanic Indiscretions of Agnes Deay*. This is a collection of stories and drawings about Belfast in 1912. They cluster round the White Star liners – 'the biggest moving objects ever built by man'.

MOLLY AND CLYDE

This story about Belfast in 1912 is set in Nevada, at Carson City, in 1901.

In 1901, on the American frontier, there was a notorious gunslinger-called John Bernard Books. J. B. Books killed more than thirty people. He survived the Wild West and outlived his century. By 1901, he was an old man, and ill. His physician, Dr Hostetler, diagnosed cancer. Books asked if he could cut the cancer out. Hostetler advised him that this was impossible. He said: 'I'd have to gut you like a fish.' Books wanted to know what his death would be like. 'If you're lucky,' said Hostetler, 'you'll lose consciousness. Until then, you'll scream.'

So Books went to Carson City to die. He took a room in a boarding house. It was run by a widow called Bond Rogers. This woman had a teenage son who thought he could make his name as a gunman.

Books was scared. He wanted privacy. But news of his arrival spread. The Marshal of Carson, Walter Thibodeaux, called. He was worried that Books would attract undesirables. 'Don't take too long to die,' he told him. 'Be a gent and convenience everybody and do it soon.'

As things turned out, Books did it in eight days. In the process he rescued his landlady's son and disillusioned him with violence. On the last day he went to the local saloon and shot three lethal desperadoes.

He was mortally wounded. But at least he died quickly.

Except, of course, that history denies it.

The saddle-tramps who mustered in the bar had been heading in that direction for centuries. The road to Carson City started in Belfast. The pioneers were Morisons from Down and Antrim.

60

These Morisons were Presbyterians. In the story of J.B. Books, there were twelve.

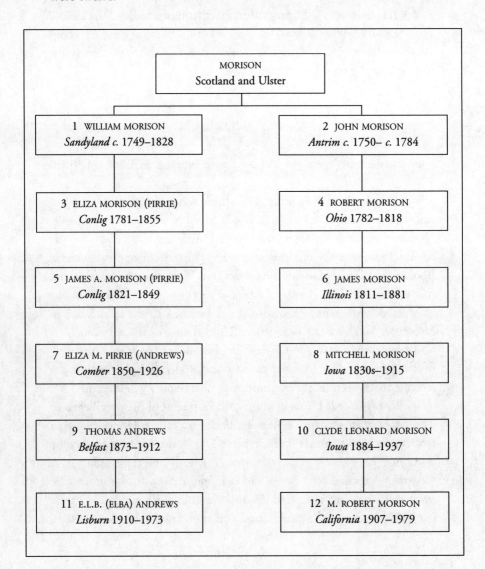

MORISON
Scotland and Ulster

1 WILLIAM MORISON
Sandyland c. 1749–1828

2 JOHN MORISON
Antrim c. 1750– c. 1784

3 ELIZA MORISON (PIRRIE)
Conlig 1781–1855

4 ROBERT MORISON
Ohio 1782–1818

5 JAMES A. MORISON (PIRRIE)
Conlig 1821–1849

6 JAMES MORISON
Illinois 1811–1881

7 ELIZA M. PIRRIE (ANDREWS)
Comber 1850–1926

8 MITCHELL MORISON
Iowa 1830s–1915

9 THOMAS ANDREWS
Belfast 1873–1912

10 CLYDE LEONARD MORISON
Iowa 1884–1937

11 E.L.B. (ELBA) ANDREWS
Lisburn 1910–1973

12 M. ROBERT MORISON
California 1907–1979

1

The first was William Morison of Sandyland. William was born about 1749. He married a girl from Conlig, near Bangor, and they raised a big family in dangerous times. The revolution in America had serious results in Ulster. It filled the place with heroes and gunslingers. The French Revolution increased the excitement. In the end, in the 1790s, there were action-packed shootouts. The last adventure was in Dublin, and the leader was hanged in 1803. His name was Robert Emmet. He was twenty-five. But William Morison of Sandyland survived. He died in 1828. His widow died in 1830. They were buried at Bangor Abbey, close to the sea.

The second was John Morrison, in County Antrim. John Morrison lived at the same time as William. Like William, he married and started a family. Like William, he heard the news from America and watched the gunmen practising in Ulster. But John died young. He missed the shootouts. He left them to his widow and his son.

The third was William of Sandyland's daughter. Eliza Morison grew up at Bangor and thought the gunplay was romantic. In 1810 she married and her surname changed to Pirrie. Her husband was a wealthy sailor from Scotland, a captain who became an American citizen. His youngest son was christened Washington. The skipper settled in Belfast, built up his business, and devoted himself to improving the harbour – he expected a lively trade with New York. In his last years he went to live at Conlig. Eliza died in 1855. Her husband died in 1858.

The fourth was John of Antrim's son. Robert Morrison was born in 1782, and brought up by his widowed mother. He thought he could make his name as a gunman. Before he was twenty, he took to the hills. In the 1790s he fought in the shootouts. When his gang was defeated, he fled to America. In 1799 he arrived in New York. He might have shared the fate of Robert Emmet. Instead, he went to Carolina, then moved to Kentucky and on to Ohio. He married in America and raised a family.

The fifth was Eliza Morison's son – James Alexander Morison Pirrie. James was born in 1821. He took himself to Canada to start a business

and married an Ulster girl in Quebec. They had a daughter and a son. In 1849, James was in New York. He caught cholera, died, and was buried at Greenwood. His widow brought the children home to Conlig.

The sixth was Robert of Ohio's son – another James. James Morrison was born in 1811. In later life he moved to Illinois. He married and brought up a large family.

The seventh was the daughter from Quebec. Eliza Morison Pirrie was born in 1845. She married a miller from Comber whose surname was Andrews. Her husband was a friend of Edward Carson, the charismatic leader of the Irish Protestants. Gunslinging was back in fashion again. This time the shootouts tore Ireland in two, and Belfast became Carson City. Eliza managed to survive. She died in 1926.

The eighth was a son of James of Illinois. Mitchell Morrison was born in the 1830s. He joined the Union Army and endured the Civil War. Afterwards he married and had children. In the 1880s he moved west to Iowa. He died in California in 1915.

The ninth was a son of Eliza of Comber. Thomas Andrews was born in 1873. He moved to Belfast and studied naval architecture. He married and had a daughter. At the same time, in his office at Harland & Wolff, he drew the biggest ships the world had ever seen. In 1912 he sailed on the *Titanic* and met a wealthy passenger called Molly Brown. On 15 April Thomas sank with his ship. But Molly Brown survived and turned into a legend – Molly was The Unsinkable Molly Brown, a heroine of Broadway and later of Hollywood. Eventually the film that was made about her arrived in Belfast and John Andrews saw it. John was the elder brother of Thomas. He followed a career in politics and became Northern Ireland's second Prime Minister.

The tenth was a son of Mitchell of Iowa. Clyde Leonard Morrison was born in 1884. In 1905 he qualified in pharmacy. In the same year he married his own Molly Brown, a lady as formidable as her maritime namesake. They started their family in Madison County. But the marriage was rocky and so was Clyde's business. By January 1912 he was bankrupt. On 15 April, when the *Titanic* went down, Clyde was chasing pennies on a dime-store counter. In the same year, his second son

was delivered. Molly called him Robert Emmett. The name reminded her of Ireland and the gunmen of 1803. Soon afterwards, Clyde moved to California. He was divorced in 1930 and married again. He died in 1937. His Molly Brown survived till 1970.

The eleventh was Thomas Andrews's daughter. Elizabeth Law Barbour Andrews was born in 1910. She was known (from her initials) as Elba. In 1917 her mother remarried. A year later, Elba danced for Lloyd George. The dance was in a room below a lake, a submarine playpen with glass in the ceiling. Elba did not marry. Eventually she settled in a house near Lisburn. She lived to see the gunmen back at work in Ulster and watched the Parliament at Stormont sinking. She was killed in a car crash in 1973.

The twelfth was a son of Molly and Clyde – the big brother of Robert Emmett Morrison. He was born in Madison County on 25 May 1907. He weighed thirteen pounds. A lifetime later, in 1976, he walked to the saloon in Carson City, shot three saddle-tramps, and died of bullets. It was his last adventure. His doctor was James Stewart and his landlady Lauren Bacall. He himself was Marion Robert Morrison, otherwise Marion Mitchell Morrison, later Marion Michael Morrison, alias Sean Thornton, Ethan Edwards, Davy Crockett, Tom Doniphon, McLintock, Rooster Cogburn, Chisum, Big Jake, Cahill, McQ, Brannigan, J.B. Books, The Shootist, Duke, and John Wayne. He died of cancer, slowly, in 1979.

Every day, everywhere, on millions of screens, the shootist falls and Mrs Rogers tends him. Hourly, on a thousand channels, the hull of the *Titanic* tilts against the stars.

If Elba's great-great-grandfather – the American skipper – had settled in New York instead of Belfast, would there ever have been a night to remember? If the Duke's great-great-grandfather – the Antrim gun-slinger – had met a J. B. Books in Ballymena, could anybody else have been John Wayne?

If Elba had been born in Madison County, she might have danced for Woodrow Wilson. If Marion had lived in Lisburn, he might have been Prime Minister of Northern Ireland.

63

READINGS

Leonard A. Morrison, *The history of the Morison or Morrison family,,* 1880

Herbert Jefferson, *Viscount Pirrie of Belfast, c.*1950

Leon O Broin, *The unfortunate Mr Robert Emmet,* 1958

Maurice Zolotow, *Shooting star : a biography of John Wayne,* 1974

P. O'Donnell, *The Irish faction fighters of the nineteenth century,* 1975

Will Wright, *Six-guns and society : a structural study of the Western,* 1975

A.C.W. Merrick & R.S.J. Clarke, *Gravestone inscriptions of County Down:* volume 17, 1978

John H. Lenihan, *Showdown: confronting modern America in the Western:* FILM, 1980

Les Adams & Buck Rainey, *Shoot-em-ups: the complete reference guide to Westerns of the sound era,* 1985

David N. Doyle Ireland, *Irishmen, and Revolutionary America,* 1991

Judith M. Riggin, *John Wayne: a bio-bibliography,* 1992

Richard Slotkin, *Gunfighter Nation: the Myth of the Frontier in Twentieth Century America,* 1992

Alvin Jackson, *Sir Edward Carson,* 1993

Randy Roberts & James S. Olson, *John Wayne: American,* 1995

A.T.Q. Stewart, *The Summer Soldiers,* 1995

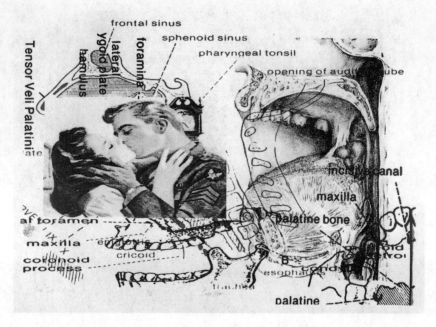

It's just a Kiss
Lithograph/screenprint
ERIC PITT
TEXAS TECH UNIVERSITY

A MAP OF OUR DREAMS
Cinema and Cultural Identity, 1955–72

SOPHIE HILLAN KING

GEORGE Are you game, Vi? Let's make a night of it.
VIOLET (just what she wanted) Oh, I'd love it, Georgie. What'll we do?
GEORGE Let's go out in the fields and take off our shoes and walk
  through the grass.
VIOLET Huh?
GEORGE Then we can go up to the falls. It's beautiful up there in the
  moonlight, and there's a green pool up there, and we can swim in it.
  Then we can climb Mt. Bedford, and smell the pines, and watch the
  sunrise against the peaks, and ... we'll stay up there the whole
  night, and everybody'll be talking and there'll be a terrific scandal...
VIOLET(interrupting) George, have you gone crazy? Walk in the grass in my
  bare feet? Why it's ten miles up to Mt. Bedford.[1]

If Woody Allen's assertion in *Annie Hall* that Diane Keaton's character grew up in a Norman Rockwell painting is true, then I grew up in
the movie quoted above, *It's a Wonderful Life.* This was Frank Capra's
1946 exploration of small-town America and its faith or lack of it in
the values of home, family and friends. James Stewart played George
Bailey, a gentle, humorous, intelligent, conscientious and deeply frustrated man unable to escape the prison of his small town, Bedford Falls.
When, in despair after an irreplaceable sum of money goes missing on
Christmas Eve, George attempts suicide, he is saved by his guardian
angel, an elderly soul named Clarence Oddbody, who dives into the
water and forces George, once more, to put someone else before himself. He then shows George what Bedford Falls would have been without him, and causes him to be grateful for his family, his friends and,

ultimately, his life. Meanwhile, all George's acquaintance rally round and replace the missing money.

Some cynics dismiss it as 'Capracorn' and, indeed, when Capra first summarised the story to returning war-hero Stewart, it seemed poor even to the teller. Stewart did not think so, and agreed to take the part.[2] In *It's A Wonderful Life*, James Stewart stopped acting the boy ranger, Jefferson Smith, of *Mr Smith Goes to Washington.* The new Stewart displayed an unsuspected range and depth, showing a boy growing into a man full of human contradiction, devoted to his family, appreciating his friends, but also seething with anger at his inability to realise all his plans and ambitions.

The film did not suit the mood of post-war America and, despite the great affection in which it continued to be held by director and star, it was quickly relegated to television, where it seemed to be shown every Christmas of my childhood. So powerful was the impression it made on me that it almost defined my view of the outside world. Part of the reason for this was that my geography, then as now, was hazy. I did not know that America was far away, or that Hollywood was not Holywood, Co. Down. Our house was at the very edge of the town, just inside the city boundary, with a farm opposite us, a dairy down the road and the remains of a threshing mill two minutes up the road, behind thatched cottages. All the houses and gardens were neat, well-tended and unassuming. We knew everyone in them, as predictable a mixture of people and walks of life as could be found in any village or small town, which is what Andersonstown then was. Behind us was a large plot, or allotment, tended by the two local policemen in their spare time: they used to come to the back fence, collarless, and hand me cabbages or rhubarb to bring in to my mother. Behind the plot were seven trees, one for each day of the week, and behind those was the Black Mountain.

When I first saw, sometime in the early fifties, *It's A Wonderful Life* on television, I simply assumed that Bedford Falls was part of Belfast. The sounds were not significantly different. When I listened to the exchange quoted at the beginning of this article, between George Bailey and one of the two women in love with him, I assumed they

were going to go up the Falls Road, to the Falls Park, just down the road from us, to have a swim in the open-air pool at the top of the park, under the shadow of the mountain which I knew as the Black Mountain, but which could just as easily have been called, for all I knew, Mount Bedford. It sounded to me a most attractive proposition, and I could not understand why Violet did not seize the opportunity.

George Bailey looked right, too. My father dressed in a suit (including waistcoat), tweed topcoat and fedora as he did, and went every morning to an office very similar to that in which George toiled – those high desks and stools, Bentwood chairs and turned hatstands, fierce black typewriters and heavy mechanical adding machines could have come out of my father's office in Donegall Place as easily as out of George's in Bedford Falls. Our office, too, was a family business, and there were uncles and family and friends enough to render the screen interpretation perfectly familiar. Under a photograph of his father in George's office was a framed motto: 'All you can take with you is what you have given away'. That, too, could have been my father's.

On the way down the Falls Road to the office, by car or trolley-bus, one would pass small and intricate shops, wonderfully lit at Christmas. There was the Broadway cinema, which we visited about once a year for the latest Disney—*Davy Crockett, King of the Wild Frontier*, or *20,000 Leagues Under the Sea*. Also on the way were our schools, the Falls library, two cemeteries where our families and people we knew were buried, and churches of all denominations: for ours was then a mixed community. It was only later that Andersonstown and the Falls Road became exclusively Catholic: at the time of which I write there were within walking distance of our house Church of Ireland, Methodist and Presbyterian churches, although I did not then know that there was any difference between ours and theirs. What I was aware of, without knowing it, was what can best be described as a sense of community. The qualities prized and praised were fidelity to family and church, courtesy, honesty, thrift and reliability: I believe it was this palpable sense of the familiar, of *pietas*, in the old sense of fidelity to tradition, that connected my home with the world created by Capra and Stewart in the movie. Asked his opinion, many years after the

69

event, about the disappointing response to the film when it was first released, James Stewart rather confirmed this impression:

> It has always been amazing to me that after the war people didn't want this story. They had been through too much. They wanted wild slapstick comedy, they wanted westerns – stuff like that. It just took a while for the country to sort of quiet down. Then we could start to think about family and community and responsibility to family and work and so on.[3]

In the light of all this, it does not surprise me that I acted as I did one day in 1955, when I was still in Junior Infants. As the consequence of a failure to listen to what the teacher had told the class on the previous day, I found myself outside the locked gates of a school inexplicably closed on a week morning. I had been left to the end of the road by my father, who drove on to his office. As I lifted my voice in lament, I became conscious of a shadow above me, and I heard a quiet voice asking me why I was crying. I looked up, and up, at a very tall man, in a tweed coat with the collar turned up and thought, with relief but without surprise: 'It's George Bailey. George will take me home.' He did. The stranger asked me if I knew the number of the trolley bus necessary to make the journey up the Falls, and when I nodded, took my hand and brought me across the road to the bus-stop. We sat in companionable silence on a long leather seat near the door and, opposite our house, we got off. He then brought me carefully across the road and handed me at our front door to my astonished mother. I never saw him again.

With hindsight, I know how dangerous this could have been: but I felt safe, and I still believe l was safe. I do not doubt that I should have been equally safe in any of the other villages that then made up Belfast. That is not to say there were not things in life that frightened me: I picked up from the programmes I saw – they were few, and strictly monitored in our house - that there had recently been a world war, and that Germans had bombed the town. I did not know that Germany was another country. In the middle of town were vast tracts of waste ground, used as car parks. They were edged with eyeless houses, in whose broken walls were remains of rooms showing strips of bedrag-

gled wall paper and blank spaces where pictures had hung. These
bombsites had been caused by the Blitz, and people had died. I developed, as a consequence, an irrational fear of Germans, and especially of
Germans in tanks coming down the road outside our house. Later, I
would read in Brian Moore's and Michael McLaverty's work of the
extraordinary camaraderie as well as the horror of the Blitz in Belfast,
and would see confirmed my early impression of the strong sense of
community. I would never, however, lose the fear of tanks, or of soldiers.

71

It seemed that the films we saw set in England - like *Mrs Miniver* –
dealt with the hardy spirit of the British during wartime, and the need
to defeat the terrible Germans. I do not think it surprising that I preferred American films - glamorous, elegant, funny musicals with Fred
Astaire and Ginger Rogers, madcap comedy with Cary Grant and
Katherine Hepburn and, of course, anything with James Stewart who,
as far as I was concerned, was a member of the family. Moreover,
Americans' voices sounded more like ours than English voices did,
which contributed to the feeling that one was on familiar ground.
When we played – I was the middle child of five – it was at cowboys
and Indians or gangsters in Chicago, but never at war as it had so
recently occurred in Europe. We never played out the relatively recent
civil war in Ireland, either, but that was not because we did not know
about it. It was rather that we did not know very much and found it
difficult to understand what we did know. In any case, this was not a
subject which we were encouraged to discuss. We knew nothing about
the IRA except that they existed, and less about the Orange Order
except that they existed and sometimes paraded past our front door on
the way to the Field at Finaghy. We did not know why they did it, and
learned in silence not to query any of it. It was just the way things were.

Thanks to cinema, what we did know, understand and act out were
such events as the American Civil War, the victorious courage of the
Union soldiers, and the desperate bravery of the Confederate force. I
did not know at the time, or for long afterward, that James Stewart's
family was among those who emigrated to America from Ulster in the
eighteenth century, and that his ancestors fought for the Union in the

72

Civil War. It would not have surprised me to learn that fact, so strong was my sense of connection between us and America. It does surprise me a little to reflect that it was not for many years that I began to consider the differences between the interpretations of the word 'Union' as used in an American and an Irish/British context, or indeed the words 'Republican' or 'Democrat'. In the 'Fifties, all that had happened in Ireland may still have been too close, too raw for discussion. If I wondered how part of Ireland was British and why there was a border and different currency when one crossed over into the 'South' (which included the most northerly county of all, Donegal), I did not know what I wanted to know by asking. That, too, was part of the way things were. When I saw Carol Reed's version of F. L. Green's novel *Odd Man Out*, about a man on the run in Belfast, it was a thrill to see the familiar territory of the Albert Clock – even with an invented marketplace around it – and the rest of the familiar town, but I did not know it was about an IRA man. The hero, Johnny McQueen, was a member of what was referred to in the film as 'the Organization' and it was never more clearly identified than that, though it was clearly meant to be the IRA. What this film did was to introduce me to Abbey actors like F.J. McCormick and W.G. Fay, the latter the original Christy Mahon in *The Playboy of the Western World*. The star of *Odd Man Out* was the silken-voiced James Mason, who had acted with MacLiammoir and Edwards at the Gate Theatre, and frightened MacLiammoir with his 'icy English smile'.[4] When I saw Carol Reed's later and better-known film, *The Third Man*, I was struck by its eerily similar atmosphere, even to the detail of a child pointing out the fugitive, first used in *Odd Man Out*. Welles, I learned in time, was also a Gate actor, which was a curiously satisfying reflection, similar in my mind to the Belfast/Bedford connection. In films like *How Green Was My Valley* I would see Sara Allgood, sister of Molly Allgood who was loved by the author of *The Playboy of the Western World*, J.M. Synge. In *Going My Way* I would encounter Barry Fitzgerald, who was, like W.G. Fay, Sara Allgood and F.J. McCormick, an Abbey actor.

Cinema – or cinema via television – became an adjunct of reading. It was never, as I hear it now described, a substitute for or an obstacle

to the pleasure of books. The film of *Our Town*, the geography of which seemed very similar to that of Bedford Falls, introduced me to the plays and novels of Thornton Wilder. John Ford's film of *The Informer* led me to Liam O'Flaherty's work, and his colourful *The Quiet Man* to the author of the original story, Maurice Walsh, an even quieter man. These films brought different worlds closer together: Dublin and England were very far away, but America was next door. Abraham Lincoln, for example, was more real to me than figures like Parnell or Michael Collins, thanks to Henry Fonda and Raymond Massey and others who portrayed the American president. Later, I owed much of my picture of him to Jim Bishop's book *The Day Lincoln was Shot* – which I read as a Reader's Digest Condensed Book one Saturday afternoon -and to Walt Whitman's 'When Lilacs Last in the Dooryard Bloomed'.[5] This poem was imbued with a double poignancy for me when read in the context of the Kennedy assassination in 1963. Kennedy himself seemed something of a cinematic hero: are we not assured that those who heard his first debate with Richard Nixon on radio assumed that Nixon had won, and that it was those who witnessed the stunningly attractive and engaging Kennedy on television who gave their support to him? I was in no doubt: Kennedy was Irish and also American. He was another star, and I was on his side from the moment I saw him. Not long ago, I heard a speech he made some months before his death in which he quoted Robert Frost's 'Choose Something Like A Star':

> It asks a little of us here.
> It asks of us a certain height,
> So when at times the mob is swayed
> To carry praise or blame too far,
> We may choose something like a star
> To stay our minds on and be staid. [6]

It occurred to me, listening to him read Frost's words, that his genius – that of the comet across the sky, wondered at and then abruptly gone – owes less to the necessarily limited achievements of his short presidency and to the unforeseen consequences not only of what he did or

73

failed to do, than to the fact that, like Robert Preston's Professor Harold Hill in *The Music Man*, a rarely shown but captivating movie, he persuaded an entire generation that they were different, special and capable of great things. He was, himself, something like a star.

With the passage of years, I find the Kennedy story more and more like a movie script, even when not linked with the movies themselves. I do not refer to the much-documented connections of the Kennedys with movie actresses, simply because so much has already been said. I find it more interesting that one of the Kennedy grandfathers, John F. Fitzgerald, defeated Jim Curley in a famous election for mayor, and that this Curley was the model for the hero of the film of Edwin O'Connor's novel *The Last Hurrah*, played by Spencer Tracy.[7] I read recently that Joseph P. Kennedy, the president's father, when U.S. Ambassador to the Court of St James, was so scandalised by the thought that James Stewart's *Mr Smith Goes to Washington* 'would be interpreted by Europeans as Nazi propaganda and put the United States in such a bad light that the morale of the British-led Allies would be seriously undermined' that he 'offered to buy the negative of the picture personally so it would be kept out of circulation'.[8] In a round-about way, this brings me to the darker side of the films I loved, including *It's a Wonderful life* itself.

By the time I was in my mid -teens, television had given to us a number of the films of the 'Fifties. I was acquainted with the harder, tougher James Stewart of Anthony Mann's westerns, and of *Vertigo*. About 1967, I saw *It's A Wonderful Life* for the first time in about ten years. Videotapes and video recorders not being then available, we were dependent upon the whims of programme planners, and I am sure it had been many years since the movie had been shown on BBC or ITV. For the first time, I was aware of the darkness at the heart of the film. George Bailey, though clearly as gifted, attractive and exceptionally good-hearted as I remembered, suddenly revealed himself to me as an embittered and angry man. Early in the film the town capitalist, Henry F. Potter, who despises the Bailey family for trying to make it possible for people to own their own homes and escape from Potter's slums, is labelled by the young George a 'warped, frustrated old man'. When

Potter, by taking advantage of George's uncle's forgetfulness and effectively stealing eight thousand dollars from the Bailey Building and Loan Society, has manoeuvred the younger man into the position of asking him for help, he takes his revenge.

> POTTER (sarcastically) Look at you. You used to be so cocky. You were going to go out and conquer the world. You once called me a warped, frustrated old man. What are you but a warped, frustrated young man? A miserable little clerk crawling in here on your hands and knees and begging for help. No securities – no stocks – no bonds – nothing but a miserable little five hundred dollar equity in a life insurance policy. ... You're worth more dead than alive. Why don't you go to the riff-raff you love so much and ask them to let you have eight thousand dollars? You know why? Because they'd run you out of town on a rail. ... But I'll tell you what I'm going to do for you, George. Since the State Examiner is here, as a stockholder of the Building and Loan, I'm going to swear out a warrant for your arrest. Misappropriation of funds – manipulation – malfeasance ...[9]

Just before this happens, George has already shocked the audience. Coming home, knowing that eight thousand dollars are missing, to his damp and draughty house full of over-excited children variously thumping out carols, blowing whistles and asking him questions, he snaps. He suddenly vents his feelings in a wanton, frenzied destruction of his own careful, detailed projects, clearly the work of months or years. For a terrible minute he destroys all he can lay his hands upon. Capra's screenplay describes it thus:

> The room has suddenly become ominously quiet, the only SOUND being George's labored breathing. George goes over to a corner of the room where his workshop is set up – a drawing table, several models of modern buildings, bridges, etc. Savagely he kicks over the models, picks up some books and hurls them into the corner, Mary and the children watch, horrified. George looks around, and sees them staring at him as if he were some unknown wild animal. The three children are crying. [10]

That sequence, culminating in his wife's asking him why he must 'torture the children' is preceded by an equally unsettling scene where he threatens his forgetful, elderly uncle:

GEORGE(screaming at him) Where's that money, you stupid, silly old fool? Where's the money? Do you realize what this means? It means bankruptcy and scandal, and prison! He throws Uncle Billy down into his chair, and still shouts at him: That's what it means! One of us is going to jail! Well, it's not going to be me! George turns and heads for the door, kicking viciously at a waste basket on the floor as he goes. Uncle Billy remains sobbing at the table, his head in his arms.[11]

It is this demented creature, not the generous, romantic, laconically humorous George, who is challenged by his unconventional guardian angel to reconsider his supposedly wasted life. It is in this context that he is persuaded to be recalled to life, even at the cost of undergoing the prospect of prison and disgrace at the hands of Potter. In return, he knows that his life, flawed and misdirected though it seems, has been worthwhile because, while unable to carry out his own ambitions, he has made it possible for others – his family, friends and colleagues – to realise theirs. The future is still dark, even when the townspeople rally and save the day by putting together their own savings to save him. The truth is that George will never leave, never see the world, never build the buildings and bridges he has designed in his head.

Such was my response in 1967. I had never noticed in the safety of childhood how bleak the underlying implications were. I believe it was at this time that I began to look for an underlying quality in film which I can describe only as grace. Fred Astaire had it. I always admired his films, but discovered only in my teens that his ease and seeming nonchalance were the product of punishing, unremitting work. I learned that Ginger Rogers bled into her shoes in order to perfect the stunningly beautiful sequence 'Never Gonna Dance' at the end of *Swing Time*. Fred, a concentrated, perfectionist genius intent upon getting it right, did not notice and Ginger, trouper to the last, did not mention it. So I began to look beyond what was apparent in films. Fred Astaire's discipline is evident in his still, almost mask-like face while he dances. Yet, he cannot always contain his joy in the form; his hands flutter like birds, almost outside himself. This is very clear in the dance which accompanies 'Night and Day' in the film *The Gay Divorce*. Wonderfully expressive hands, in constant nervous motion,

are a feature, too, of James Stewart's best work. Like Astaire's, his hands are held like captive birds, carried at times as though injured; indeed, in *The Man From Laramie*, one of them is, quite brutally, by a pistol fired at close range. I began to notice the elegance of Stewart's movements, the economy with which he manoeuvres a very tall frame quickly and gracefully. I wondered why he chose to parody himself in later performances, when, in films from *The Shop Around the Corner* to *It's A Wonderful Life*, he showed that he could move like a dancer. In fact, Ginger Rogers once said that he was a better dancer than Fred Astaire – but that may have been because she was not bleeding into her shoes at the time. Yet, Capra saw and caught the perfectionist, near-neurotic side of Stewart in *It's a Wonderful Life*.

77

At the time the film was being made, Stewart, just returned from the war, was far from sure about his future, and doubted whether there was much value in being a movie actor. It took Lionel Barrymore, who played – against type – the evil and destructive Potter, to persuade him that what he was doing was just as valuable as fighting a war. Capra recalls it thus:

> A few days later Barrymore talked to Jimmy and gave him a pitch on acting that would have convinced just about anyone: 'Don't you realize,' he said, 'that you're moving millions of people, shaping their lives, giving them a sense of exaltation. What other profession has that power or can be so important? A bad actor is a bad actor. But acting is among the oldest and noblest professions in the world, young man.' Stewart took due note of the advice. He never actually said it in so many words, but I think it was from that moment that Jimmy decided that if he was going to be an actor, then he was going to be the best there was.[12]

Meanwhile, Capra wanted a central romantic scene, where George realises that, though he cannot escape Bedford Falls, there is much that he wants and needs there – primarily Mary Hatch, the young girl (played by Donna Reed) who has loved him since they were children. According to one publicity release, Stewart asked Capra to delay the great screen embrace because, as he put it, 'a fellow's technique gets rusty'. The director would have none of this and 'to make sure Jimmy would not bolt, Capra huddled his stars over a telephone, conducting

78

a conversation with Frank Albertson, who wants to marry Donna in the picture. Jimmy was raining perspiration, but he began playing the scene with tense urgency'. As Donna Reed responded to his mood, 'Stewart flung the telephone away and really gave it everything in high gear'. Capra was delighted, despite the fact that his script girl pointed out that 'it was fine all right, except that they left out a whole page of dialogue'. The release gives Capra's reply: 'With technique like that,' he said, 'who needs dialogue? Print it!'[13] So startling, in fact, was the technique, that the sequence was almost cut by the censor. A still of the scene exists on which, in scrawled handwriting, rests the legend: 'Killed. Johnston office'.[14]

The kind of grace to which I refer exists in the work of many actors. I think of James Mason in *Lolita*, for example; of Burt Lancaster in *The Leopard*; of the Hepburns, Katharine and Audrey; of Spencer Tracy, Cary Grant, Henry Fonda and Humphrey Bogart and, today, of Meryl Streep, Robert de Niro and Ralph Fiennes. At the time of which I write, the late sixties, I was not aware of all that there was to be found in cinema. It came to me in glimpses, in *It's A Wonderful Life*, or in such films as *The Night of the Hunter*, the only work directed by Charles Laughton, starring Robert Mitchum, who was considered by Laughton 'one of the best actors in the world'.[15] Laughton, wrote a recent critic, 'saw beneath Mitchum's surpassing cool the heat of an often disappointed perfectionist'.[16] I found myself fascinated and appalled by Mitchum's psychopathic preacher, the words 'love' and 'hate' tattooed on his knuckles, going about the ruthless pursuit of two children who know where stolen money is hidden, and whose mother he has murdered. Yet, it was a beautiful film, deeply sympathetic to the fractured world of the lonely children. Delicate camera work included a dream-like sequence in which the children drift down the river, while the gentle voice of Lillian Gish tells the story of the child Moses. Looking out from their haven, a warm dry barn for the night, they see the terrible figure of the preacher in silhouette against the horizon, his dark, rich voice singing a hymn soothing as a lullaby. I cannot help connecting these two apparently different films, each one part fairytale, two parts nightmare. *The Night of the Hunter* was made in the very year when I

was entrusting my hand to a stranger, and Mitchum and Stewart, both of whom were revealed to me as nowhere else by these two films, died within a day of each other last summer. After their deaths, one American critic wrote:

> Recently people have been asking me who I liked better, Jimmy Stewart or Robert Mitchum. I wouldn't play the game. They were both one of a kind. Each had a style, a grace, a bearing, a voice, a face, a walk that were unmistakeable and irreplaceable …
>
> So, Mitchum or Stewart? I cannot choose. I cannot do without either one of them. They are among the immortals. But when Stewart died, the entire nation went into mourning, and the president issued a statement, which he had not been moved to do the day before. And I thought, yes, all honor to Jimmy. But let us also love and remember Mitch. And I put on my laser disc of 'Night of the Hunter' and listened to Mitchum's voice coiling from the screen ('Chill…dren?').And I thought, Stewart was the heart, and Mitchum was the soul.[17]

Meanwhile, as I began to have some sense beyond the instinctive of the beauty and significance of cinema, my own world had changed but little. Until 1967, trolley buses still ran on the Falls Road; the building of Divis Flats and the compulsory relocating of people from the terraced houses of the Lower Falls to what would become notorious estates on the outskirts of the city had not quite begun. The Beatles had come and gone in 1963, and Stormont was still ruling our lives.

In 1968, as significant a year of revolutions as 1848 had been for another generation, I went to Queen's University on the other side of the town – my first foray away from the sheltered world of youth. Martin Luther King and Robert Kennedy were dead, and students, little older than we were, had brought Paris to a standstill. A spirit of unrest – exciting, almost tangible – was in the air. Over the next few months, my life changed more than it had in the previous eighteen. I met people from different schools and, for the first time, people who were not Catholic. The University represented a whole new world, and it seemed to me everything I had hoped for. I was there to read and to learn, perhaps to write, and I was with people who were there for the same purpose. In the English Department, we were wonderfully taught

by, among others, Seamus Heaney, who held our complete attention in lectures and talked to us like adults outside. We were in a University in the forefront of Irish Studies – the geographer and archaeologist Estyn Evans had in 1965 founded in Queens the first ever Institute of Irish Studies, dedicated to scholarship in any discipline relating to Ireland. Beside me in lectures were the poet Medbh McGuckian and future *Irish Times* journalist Conor O'Clery, while another poet, Paul Muldoon, was to come along in the following year. Writing and living in the town were such figures as Michael McLaverty, whose novels and stories described the very streets and houses I had passed on the way to school. At the BBC was Sam Hanna Bell, who had himself caught in novels and short stories the fast-disappearing customs of Ulster life. It was a good time to be a student.

In my first year we studied twentieth century literature – Joyce, Lawrence, Yeats, Conrad, Louis MacNeice. About Christmas, I came across E.M. Forster's *Collected Short Stories*. It contained a story to which I constantly return, 'The Celestial Omnibus', about a child whom no-one believes when he tells them he has gone to heaven and back on a bus, driven by Jane Austen, and has met there all the heroes of literature and legend. Chief among the sceptics is a family friend, Mr Bons, who is full of bombast and does not really care for literature: when he tests out the boy, he is given his ride on the bus, driven this time by a grim-faced Dante Alighieri and, while the child is raised to heroic status by Achilles himself, and assumed into heaven, the sceptical Mr Bons is hurled to cruel death for his unbelief and pompous pretence:

> The last fragment of the rainbow melted, the wheels sang upon the living rock, the door of the omnibus burst open. Out leapt the boy – he could not resist – and sprang to meet the warrior, who, stooping suddenly, caught him on his shield.
>
> 'Achilles!' he cried, 'let me get down, for I am ignorant and vulgar, and I must wait for that Mr Bons of whom I told you yesterday.' But Achilles raised him aloft. He crouched on the wonderful shield, on heroes and burning cities, on vineyards graven in gold, on every dear passion, every joy, on the entire image of the Mountain that he had discovered,

encircled, like it, with an everlasting stream. 'No, no,' he protested, 'I am not worthy. It is Mr Bons who must be up here.'

But Mr Bons was whimpering, and Achilles trumpeted and cried, 'Stand upright on my shield!' 'Sir, I did not mean to stand! Something made me stand. Sir, why do you delay? Here is only the great Achilles, whom you knew.' Mr Bons screamed, 'I see no-one. I see nothing. I want to go back.' Then he cried to the driver, 'Save me! Let me stop in your chariot. I have honoured you. I have quoted you. I have bound you in vellum. Take me back to my world.'

The driver replied, 'I am the means and not the end. I am the food and not the life. Stand by yourself, as that boy has stood. I cannot save you. For poetry is a spirit; and they that would worship it must worship in spirit and in truth.'

Mr Bons — he could not resist – crawled out of the beautiful omnibus. His face appeared, gaping horribly. His hands followed, one gripping the step, the other beating the air. Now his shoulders emerged, his chest, his stomach. With a shriek of 'I see London,' he fell – fell against the hard, moonlit rock, fell into it as if it were water, fell through it, vanished, and was seen by the boy no more. [18]

Like the films described above, absorbed at a receptive time, this story had a profound effect upon me. It was not simply that it contained echoes of so much that I had read – children's versions of Homer and Dante, Tennyson's 'Ulysses' and Jane Austen's novels. What struck me was the dawning realisation that it was not enough to want to read literature: I had to be able to read it at several levels at once, to think my way in and around and out of it, all of which was much more difficult. It was a matter of perfectionism again, of bleeding in the shoes.

Study became at once more difficult and more satisfying. Throughout the four years of my undergraduate degree, I moved away from the general to the particular – to Irish Studies, with an interest always in the connections with European, Scottish and American literature – all inextricably linked by history and experience. On the way, I moved through Anglo-Saxon and mediaeval literature, the Renaissance, the age of the Augustans and the Romantics, spending time with Dr Johnson and Oliver Goldsmith, with Jane Austen, with Sir Walter Scott and Maria Edgeworth, Shelley, Keats and Charles

Dickens. When I came to my final year, I had the opportunity to study American literature as an option, and rediscovered, with a shock, the world of Bedford Falls in Thornton Wilder's *Our Town*. In his preface, Wilder wrote:

82

> *Our Town* is not offered as a picture of life in a New Hampshire village; or as a speculation about the conditions of life after death. It is an attempt to find a value above all price for the smallest events in our daily life.[19]

In *Our Town*, a woman who has died young is given the chance to relive one day, an unimportant day, in her earthly life. She chooses her twelfth birthday, and witnesses a Bedford Falls kind of day – the reverse of the nightmare vision George is vouchsafed when he wishes he had never been born. The woman, Emily, realises the value of all the little things, the small moments, which passed without her noticing. She finds it unbearable, and begs to return to the world of the dead:

> I didn't realize. So all that was going on and we never noticed. Take me back—up the hill—to my grave. But first: Wait! One more look. Goodbye, Goodbye world. Goodbye, Grover's Corners ... Mama and Papa. Good-bye to clocks ticking ... and Mama's sunflowers. And food and coffee. And new-ironed dresses and hot baths ... and sleeping and waking up. Oh, earth, you're too wonderful for anybody to realize you.[20]

The only difference between Emily's experience and that of George Bailey is that George realises before death, 'the value above all price [of] the smallest events in our daily life'. I found a similar sense of world become precious at the moment of its passing in Emily Dickinson, especially in the poem which begins, 'Because I could not stop for death', ending with the words:

> Since then 'tis centuries; but each
> Feels shorter than the day
> I first surmised the horses' heads
> Were toward eternity. [21]

I discovered this sense again, many years after the time of which I now write, in William Kennedy's novel, *Ironweed*. In the opening sequence, Francis Phelan finds himself in the cemetery where many of his

relatives, including the baby son whose death he brought about by carelessness, observe him, cool and detached, from their graves.[22] It was with a sense of recognition that I remembered, not only Wilder and Dickinson, but also Bedford Falls, where George in his nightmare vision sees the grave of the little brother he was not alive to save, and who could not then grow up to become the war hero of George's benign, despised life. Recently, I saw the film of *Ironweed*, so faithfully and movingly acted by Jack Nicholson and Meryl Streep that it was an immediate failure at the box office (just like *It's a Wonderful Life*). I could not help noticing that the opening sequence, a panorama of stars in the vast night sky, was uncannily similar to the opening of *It's A Wonderful Life*. The difference was that, as the camera moved down to life on earth, the protagonists in this film were already living their nightmare, on the streets of 'Thirties America. They had ghosts and visions enough; there was no-one to guide them but themselves and their sad, enduring love; yet the film recalls for me, irresistibly, Capra's and Stewart's great movie.

The development of my response to cinema was gradual. It was just beginning to happen in the late 'Sixties when I was, for the first time, surrounded by the most dramatic kind of politics which, like the study of literature, seemed to demand of me something approaching understanding, if not involvement. I was not politically aware. Living at home and a much protected girl, who was expected to come in by eleven accompanied by at least one and preferably two brothers, I was not encouraged to participate in anything political, and indeed was not temperamentally suited to rebellion of any kind – unless I could read about it or watch it on screen. Yet, I knew or knew of those who were so suited, and could not ignore the fact that history was taking place on the doorstep of the university. I remember the day in the first term of my first year when many of my fellow students sat down outside the City Hall and were puzzled, astonished and disillusioned by the incredible fact that they were being blocked from demonstrating in favour of Civil Rights by policemen in riot gear: that was the night that People's Democracy was formed. Eilis McDermott, whom I did not then know but who was my exact contemporary at the university, has described

precisely the way in which the climate of anger after Burntollet in
January 1969 turned into the fullscale violence of 1969 and thereafter:

> But the rage which had been burning in loyalist areas erupted in August
> 1969. Tension had been building up for days. I was in Albert Street in the
> Lower Falls area of Belfast, by myself, when the shooting started. A
> woman pulled me in her door and, despite a pathological fear of dogs, I
> lay on the floor clutching her labrador. She had recognised me from see-
> ing me on television. She would not let me go until she thought it was
> safe and as she let me out, she said: 'Look what you've started, daughter'.
> I ran back to Queen's feeling bitterly angry and ashamed. I knew we had
> not 'started' anything and I knew she had not meant it that way, but there
> was something very shaming about having been involved in some way in
> defenceless people being shot dead. No one was shooting in University
> Road. [23]

Before I left the university, people were shooting on University Road,
and the houses I knew, the Falls Road of my childhood and the little
houses described by Michael McLaverty, in which Eilis McDermott
took shelter, had disappeared for ever. I saw on a quiet summer morning the tanks of my early nightmare roll down the road in front of my
house, manned not by German, but by British soldiers. Children, no
bigger than we had been in the 'Fifties, set fire to the seven trees behind
our house, leaving blackened stumps and an empty sky. People we
knew went into a restaurant or a bus-station and were blown to pieces.
The very buses which had so often carried us home burned like sad
beacons at the side of the road. Our country police station became a
monstrous fortress, a place of barbed wire and corrugated iron. Before
I graduated from Queen's University, I had lost the illusions of youth
and had ceased to think the world a good place.

Yet, I rediscovered the relief of retreat into the world not only of
books but of cinema, no longer a mirror of the world but a necessary
safety valve. I have never cared for films which showed the blood and
entrails of those who were shot or maimed: in Belfast in the early seventies it was all too possible to see the real thing. I preferred Fellini and
Bunuel, and M. Hulot, all to be found in the haven of the Queen's
Film Theatre, in a mews behind University Square. Once, coming out

of Bunuel's *The Exterminating Angel* to a world suddenly and unexpectedly covered in snow, I did not know whether I had been assumed into the the film or had re-entered the ordinary world I had left. This strange and compelling film has been described by Bunuel himself as 'the story of a group of friends who have dinner together after seeing a play, but when they go into the living room after dinner, they find that for some inexplicable reason they can't leave'.[24] I did not immediately connect my fascination with this film with my regard for *It's a Wonderful Life*, until I read Bunuel's autobiography, in which he says of *The Exterminating Angel*: 'Basically, I simply see a group of people who couldn't do what they wanted to – leave a room. That kind of dilemma, the impossibility of satisfying a simple desire, often occurs in my movies'.[25]

85

Reading that, I saw the connection between those who cannot leave a room and the man who cannot leave his home town. On the night that I came out into the snow-covered world, I did not know whether I had entered the kind of parallel universe used to powerful effect by Flann O'Brien in *At Swim-Two-Birds* and *The Third Policeman*, but I remember the strength of the feeling of displacement. The metaphor, the query in the mind about the wisdom or danger of re-entering a supposedly known universe, is an apt one for the strange and disturbing time of the early 'Seventies in Belfast. Between the years of 1968, when I entered the university and 1972, when I graduated, the world I had known seemed to disintegrate. I did not fully understand it at the time but, nonetheless, it was happening.

Political developments, and town planning, ensured that the old Falls Road was swept away in the late 'Sixties. A new generation, angry and dispossessed, was emerging: people from the Falls were no longer content to shop in cautious camaraderie on the Shankill, or people from the Shankill on the Falls. It became dangerous to go out at night. In the summer of 1971, I could not get home on the evening after internment was introduced because of fires and shooting. I made my way to my father's office, now removed from the town and situated near the University. We walked a good deal of the way home, though my father was not young. At the bottom of Kennedy Way, a passing stranger said conversationally to my father: 'Do you see those lads there?' We saw some young men running over the plot where the policemen had tended the vegetables. 'They're the IRA'. I was amazed. That was what they looked like: boys in jeans.

86

Returning to the University for my final year in the autumn of 1971, I found a complete change in atmosphere: there was great tension, palpable fear. All the excitement of 1968 had gone. I could no longer live at home: it was too dangerous to travel across town. Then, at the very end of January in 1972, British paratrooopers opened fire on unarmed protesters in Derry. We – my friends and I – were appalled. We were even more shocked and demoralised when it emerged that throughout the University a great polarisation occurred, so that even the academic community, till then as safe as home, as houses, was fractured. After that, some stayed, but many of us left.

I was one of those who left, and did not return, except to visit family, for a long time. Yet, I came back, with my husband and small children, specifically for his job but, at some deeper level, for the sake of the town and the way of life I remembered. I thought and still think it a good place to bring up children. I began to work in the Institute of Irish Studies, among a community of scholars dedicated to research in all aspects of life on the island of Ireland. In the Institute, it became possible to hope once more that all the small and great things that are valuable about life here could be brought together to make some kind of future.

What of the movies in all this? What of Bedford Falls? In the midst of all that I describe, the precison and clarity of the movies of the 'Thirties, 'Forties and 'Fifties became even more important. When I came to read David Thomson's remarkable and disturbing novel, *Suspects*, in the late 'Eighties, I found George Bailey again. Thomson's vision of what could have happened to him – that he might have become an ill-tempered, disappointed recluse – is upsetting, but the way in which he connects all the movies I knew and admired is astonishing. Like Forster in 'The Celestial Omnibus', he challenges himself and the reader:

Is this a novel, or a non-fiction book about movies? My answer must be both. It is film criticism and movie history, but it is a fiction in which the material(the life) is the world created in a genre of movies. This is not just a way of warning readers of the rules of the game. It is a reminder that fiction has no hold unless we believe in it, and that movies use the exact poignant imprint of so many glances and faces to make a dream. So try to read without having to slap me, and ask how much your own 'real experience' treasures imaginary beings and absurd possibilities.[26]

87

His George Bailey tells us that 'the screen is like a map for our dreams on which we may always travel, without ticket, tiredness or pain. It is our greatest frontier, like a magic mirror'.[27]

I have found in the movies, as in novels and poetry, a map for my own dreams. I know now about the darkness in George Bailey, so vividly and disturbingly explored by Thomson, and still find him not only an irresistibly attractive character, but also a kind of objective correlative for survival in the Ireland we have inherited. It is possible to find the America I thought I knew: the America of the mind. George cannot escape Bedford Falls, and we cannot escape Belfast. Bedford Falls, as more than one critic has pointed out, may have a real counterpart in New York state, but the Falls Road of my childhood is no longer there, except in the minds of those who knew it. [28]

What has not passed away is the spirit that informed the Falls Road I remember. The message of the celestial messenger to George Bailey is that 'no man is a failure who has friends'. George is bitterly frustrated and angry at the very people whom he must support. He does not want to do it: he does it. Like Beckett's Unnamable, he can't go on: he goes on. Like the hero of Ambrose Bierce's 'An Occurrence at Owl Creek Bridge', as American critic James MacKillop has pointed out, he finds in the dream time between life and death that life is unbearably precious.[29] He wants to give up, but may not: in the end, in spite of himself, the regard and patience of family and friends, and the respect accorded to him for having kept going in the face of adversity, carry him through. The spirit of Capra's and Stewart's George Bailey is entirely relevant to the world we may hope to build in Belfast and beyond. Faith or lack of it in the work, as demonstrated by Forster and

in a different context by Thomson, is what is important. James Mason, writing in 1981, commented about acting itself that 'the skills of an actor should not be confined to the teaching of one school but, given intelligence and imagination, there should be no limit to his reach, even though his grasp may fall short'.[30] Mason knew it: so did James Stewart, Robert Mitchum, Fred Astaire and Ginger Rogers, who bled for the principle. Robert Frost and John F. Kennedy were fully aware of the need for 'something like a star'. My imagination needs such people, and it needs the 'imaginary beings and absurd possibilities' of the old movies, of literature and poetry to sustain it, in order to survive from day to day.

If and when my celestial omnibus arrives, and if I am not hurled into hell for having got it wrong, I cherish the hope that my guide to the other world may be George Bailey and that, along the old Falls Road which no longer exists, but which I see clearly in memory and imagination, he will once more bring me home.

REFERENCES

All references are to the editions used by the author of this article)

1   Jeanine Basinger, *It's a Wonderful Life Book* (New York: Alfred Knopf, 1986), pp.181-82.

2   Basinger, pp. 77-78; Roy Pickard, *James Stewart: The Hollywood Years* (London: Robert Hale, 1997), pp.67-68.

3   Basinger, p. 84.

4   Micheal MacLiammoir, *All For Hecuba: An Irish Theatrical Autobiography* (Dublin: Progress House, 1961), p. 195.

5   Jim Bishop, *The Day Lincoln Was Shot*, in Reader's Digest Condensed Books, vol.21, (Pleasantville, N.Y.: Reader's Digest Association, Spring 1955); Walt Whitman, *Leaves of Grass* (New York: NEL, 1958), p.265.

6   'Choose Something Like A Star', *Robert Frost: Selected Poems* (Harmondsworth: Penguin, 1966), p.251.

7   Edwin O'Connor, *The Last Hurrah* (Boston: Little, Brown and Company, 1956)

88

8   Donald Dewey, *James Stewart: A Biography* (Atlanta, Georgia: Turner Publishing, 1996), p. 195.

9   Basinger, p. 267.

10   Basinger, pp. 263–64.

11   Basinger, pp. 252–53.

12   Pickard, p. 69.

13   Basinger, pp.39–40.

14   Basinger, pp.39–40.

15   Richard Schickel, 'Eternally Cool: Robert Mitchum 1917-1997', *Time*, 14 July1997, p.55.

16   Schickel, p. 5 5 .

17   Roger Ebert, 'Immortals Both', *New York Herald Journal*, (Summer 1997).

18   E.M.Forster, *Collected Short Stories* (Harmondsworth:Penguin,1965), pp.57-58.

19   Thomton Wilder, *Our Town; The Skin of our Teeth, The Matchmaker* (Harmondsworth: Penguin, 1974), p.12.

20   Wilder, p. 89.

21   Emily Dickinson, *The Collected Poems* (New York: Barnes and Noble,1993), p.195.

22   William Kennedy, *Ironweed* (Harmondsworth: Penguin, 1985), pp.16-20.

23   Eilis McDermott, 'Law and Disorder', *Twenty Years On*, ed. by Michael Farrell (Dingle, Co.Kerry: Brandon, 1988), p. 152.

24   Luis Bunuel, *My Last Breath* (London: Jonathan Cape, 1984), p.238.

25   Bunuel, pp. 2 3 9-40.

26   David Thomson, *Suspects* (London: Pan, 1986), Preface.

27   Thomson, p.263.

28   James MacKillop, 'Bedford Falls Revisited: The Dark Side of *It's a Wonderful Life*', *Syracuse New Times*, 20 December 1989, p.9; Fran Caraccilo, 'Official: "Wonderful Life" Really Set in Seneca Falls', *The Post-Standard*, 2 August 1996, pp.Cl-2.

29   James MacKillop, in conversation with Sophia King, June 1995.

30   James Mason, *Before I Forget* (London: Hamish Hamilton, 1981), p.304.

A PERPETUAL ONE-NIGHT STAND
Some Thoughts on Jazz and Poetry

MICHAEL LONGLEY

I can remember the exact moment when the wonders of jazz first grabbed me as a young boy. The English Number One tennis player, Tony Mottram, chose as one of his Desert Island discs Fats Waller's 'Alligator Crawl'. I was standing in our kitchen at the time (early nineteen fifties?), and thrilled to the rolling boogie base of the great stride pianist. As an adolescent I first fell in love with the romantic classics, Tchaikovsky, Rachmaninov, Chopin, Grieg. In the Sixth Form at Inst I was one of a small group of highbrows who met in each other's homes to listen to the still newfangled long playing records, some of them jazz. George Filor favoured Duke Wellington, Terry Gillespie the Modern Jazz Quartet. The traditional jazz revival of the Fifties meant jiving on Saturday nights to Jimmy Compton's Band. (At the Inst hops there were 'Jitterbugging Forbidden' notices on the walls.). Chris Barber's Dixieland version of 'Bobby Shafto' was all the rage; and his guitarist Lonnie Donegan went on to become the King of Skiffle, an early example of the pop star/teenage idol phenomenon. But I was spending my pocket money on records of classical music and regularly attending concerts given by the City of Belfast Symphony Orchestra in the Ulster Hall.

At Trinity College Dublin jazz was occasionally on the menu but not yet a major preoccupation. I enjoyed some fairly modern stuff in Harry Gilmore's rooms. (Harry, who liked to play along with his records on a muted trumpet, was a Miles Davis devotee.) Johnnie Wadham, a fellow student and already a thrilling drummer, could be heard beating it out in some of the Dublin dives. My total conversion to jazz came in my twenty-fifth year when marriage and our return to Belfast

92

coincided with my discovery of Solly Lipsitz's celebrated emporium in High Street. Atlantic Records sported no shop front. With the entrance to this dusty cubbyhole at the end of a dark passageway and Solly not always in residence, one felt honoured and rather enterprising to be seated on a stool in one of the happiest atmospheres I have ever known – combative conversation, cigar smoke, gossip, jokes, new boxes of records, jazz.

My first purchase was two LPs, *Fats on the Air*, compilations of Fats Waller's radio work recorded on magnetic tapes. These made more room for the expansiveness of this larger-than-life, charismatic show-man than the three or so minutes of the oldfashioned 78s. I loved the drive, the warmth, the apparent spontaneity, the insouciance, the dizzy humour, the hilarious demolition of sentimental material, but I also sensed a dark and unsettling aspect, as though behind the twinkle Waller is issuing a challenge: "Yes, I'll make you laugh and tap your feet, folks, but not until you've kissed my fat black ass!" Waller seam-lessly combines sunniness and subversion. Undermining not only the inane Tin Pan Alley lyrics, but our racial and artistic preconceptions as well, he can be very complicated indeed. Sometimes I wish he had per-formed more often with musicians of his own calibre; that he had left us more of those tracks on which he keeps his mouth shut and just plays as a driving session man or as the composer of intricate parlour pieces like 'Handful of Keys', 'Clothesline Ballet', 'Jitterbug Waltz'. But most of the time I'm happy like everyone else to chuckle when Fats Waller sings and jokes. Ebullient perennials like 'Ain't Misbehavin' and 'Honeysuckle Rose' never fail to thrill me. To quote Louis Armstrong: "Every time someone mentions Fats Waller's name, why you can see the grins on all the faces, as if to say, 'Yea, yea, yea, yea, Fats is a solid sender, ain't he?'"

In my first collection, *No Continuing City*, I included a sequence of jazz poems called 'Words for Jazz Perhaps' and dedicated it to Solly Lipsitz. (I cheekily pinched the title from Yeats.) In the first of these, 'Elegy for Fats Waller', I refer to the rumbustious life-style which sure-ly contributed to his death at the grimly early age of thirty-nine. I try to convey the weightless artistry of this hugely overweight man. I take

him seriously, but in a way I hope he would have appreciated. His closest friends called him Thomas rather than Fats:

> Lighting up, lest all our hearts should break,
> His fiftieth cigarette of the day,
> Happy with so many notes at his beck
> And call, he sits there taking it away,
> The maker of immaculate slapstick.
>
> With music and with such precise rampage
> Across the deserts of the blues a trail
> He blazes, towards the one true mirage,
> Enormous on a nimble-footed camel
> And almost refusing to be his age.
>
> He plays for hours on end and though there be
> Oases one part water, two parts gin,
> He tumbles past to reign, wise and thirsty,
> At the still centre of his loud dominion –
> THE SHOOK THE SHAKE THE SHEIKH OF ARABY.

Or, as James P. Johnson put it in an impromptu obituary: "Some little people has music in them, but Fats, he was all music, and you know how big he was." The last line of my elegy quotes his own rendition of 'The Sheikh'. The twelfth line is historically, though not poetically, inaccurate. Waller diluted his gin with port. Love of Waller's stride playing led me to other jazz pianists: his instructor James P. Johnson who brought together ragtime and classical techniques and got the world dancing the Charleston; Art Tatum who as jazz's most prodigious virtuoso pianist was admired by Rachmaninov and Horovitz; Earl Hines whom I first heard competing with Louis Armstrong for elbow room on the later Hot Five recordings from the late Twenties; and then – miraculously – in 1966 he dazzled a few dozen of us in the Ulster Hall, an embarrassingly small audience for an artistic giant who over the decades had jousted with most of the greats. The bounce and zing of Earl Hines's improvisations brought tears to my eyes.

Round about this time the Queen's University Festival invited Bud

94

Freeman to Belfast. He performed with an English outfit, the Alex Welsh Jazz Band, and more or less filled the Whitla Hall. With his bristly pert moustache this tubby little white man in a grey suit looked more like a vacuum cleaner salesman than a hot saxophonist. He played music that veered from the hardboiled to the brittle and bitter-sweet, in the 'Chicago style', the fruit of the creative collision of black musicians who had migrated there from the south, with white disciples such as Muggsy Spanier, Eddie Condon, Mezz Mezzrow who copied and modified the classic New Orleans sound. Later, tracking down Freeman on various recordings, I uncovered further riches, the tense holler of Max Kaminsky's trumpet, the introverted, sceptical, queru-lous searchings of Pee Wee Russell's clarinet. In the mean time I wrote 'Bud Freeman in Belfast', the second poem in my jazz suite:

> Fog horn and factory siren intercept
> Each fragile hoarded-up refrain. What else
> Is there to do but let those notes erupt
>
> Until your fading last glissando settles
> Among all other sounds – carefully wrapped
> In the cotton wool from aspirin bottles?

Harry Chambers, who edited the still undervalued literary magazine, *Phoenix* (there was a special Northern Irish issue featuring poems by Heaney, Mahon, Simmons and myself, with drawings by Carolyn Mulholland), and who later founded the Peterloo Press, was living in Belfast in the Sixties. He loved jazz nearly as much as I did. The copy of Louis MacNeice's autobiography, *The Strings are False*, which Harry gave to me, is inscribed in green biro with four lines composed in my honour. Harry's quatrain catches the spirit of those days:

> I see you smiling, fat, dressed all in brown:
> Here you are mimicking that piano jazz,
> Here you are swaying on my midnight hearth
> Or quoting Irish poetry as the Scotch goes down.

At a party in Harry's flat in Camden Street the music issued from a tinny-sounding portable Dansette record player. I could just pick out

through the crush and chatter a heartstopping voice, a rich contralto, one of the most majestic sounds in all music:

> It's raining and it's storming on the sea,
> It's raining, it's storming on the sea;
> I feel like somebody has shipwrecked poor me.

95

The following day I rushed to Atlantic Records and asked for Bessie Smith albums. Solly told me that Philips had – disgracefully – deleted her from their catalogue. I asked him to order the Columbia set of five LPs from America. (Philip Larkin through his influential jazz column in the *Daily Telegraph* helped to persuade Philips to re-issue Bessie Smith some time later.)

It is a miracle how backwoods keening, mainly by men, about sex and betrayal, money and hard times, was transformed by female singers with powerful voices into a universal lamentation, a sound that would encircle the globe. Bessie Smith and other blues singers – Ma Rainey, Chippie Hill, Alberta Hunter – travelled the Southern states providing entertainment in tent shows and on vaudeville stages. Did she realise she was producing great art? The saxophonist Buster Bailey suggests: "For Bessie singing was just a living. She didn't consider it anything special." The three minute span of those early pre-electric recordings clearly helped to concentrate an already potent brew. Bessie Smith came at just the right time, a delta into which tributaries flowed - the blues, ragtime, vaudeville, Tin Pan Alley, spirituals, New Orleans jazz, jazz from Chicago and New York, a developing record industry. But nothing can really explain the glory of her achievment, the golden period of six years or so when she performed to the highest level on dozens of tracks. Even in her bawdy, obstreperous, more knock-about modes her majesty seldom deserts her. She has earned her title, 'Empress of the Blues'. When the youthful Louis Armstrong accompanies her in W.C. Handy's 'St Louis Blues' (which is for anyone who hears it the definitive version), 'Reckless Blues', 'Sobbin' Hearted Blues', 'Cold in Hand Blues', 'Careless Love', the two geniuses generate an almost unbearable electric charge. In my third poem, 'To Bessie Smith', I try to keep in mind the intensity and pathos of her music, her courage and defiance ("I ain't goodlookin' but I'm somebody's angel child"), the sexual surge of her voice, the elemental force of her personality:

> You bring from Chattanooga Tennessee
> Your huge voice to the back of my mind
> Where, like sea shells salvaged from the sea
> As bright reminders of a few weeks' stay,
> Some random notes are all I ever find.
> I couldn't play your records every day.
>
> I think of Tra-na-rossan, Inisheer,
> Of Harris drenched by horizontal rain –
> Those landscapes I must visit year by year.
> I do not live with sounds so seasonal
> Nor set up house for good. Your blues contain
> Each longed-for holiday, each terminal.

The legendary cornetist Bix Beiderbecke came from a white middle-class family who lived in Davenport on the Mississipi. As a teenager he listened to Bessie Smith, King Oliver, Louis Armstrong and at the deepest level took them all in. But he educated himself by playing over and over again records of the white ensemble The Original Dixieland Jazz Band, and in particular their cornetist Nick La Rocca. (It's ironical that the very first jazz records were cut by these white musicians in 1917.) From the beginning his cornet sings out from the dimly recorded tum-te-tum throb of a youthful group called the Wolverines. Mezz Mezzrow captures the Beiderbecke magic: "He played mostly open horn, every note full, big, rich and round, standing out like a pearl, loud but never irritating or jangling, with a powerful drive that few white musicians had in those days." At the end of his brief career (he died of alcoholism at twenty-eight) Bix was playing with the Paul Whiteman Orchestra, and scattered his pearls in pretty boring sludge. The Whiteman recordings survive only because Bix made his immortal contribution, hot breaks that are tantalisingly brief, sometimes only several seconds long, miniature versions of the story of his life. To the modified Dixieland style he brought a melodic line that even at its loveliest never sacrifices tension, and a rhythmic propulsion that can be

rapturous without overwhelming an essential note of sadness. Tracks like 'Singin' the Blues' and 'I'm Comin', Virginia' delight me as much as any music. Bix Beiderbecke was the first white man to play great jazz. My parents came from London to live in Belfast. When I wrote 'To Bix Beiderbecke' in my mid-twenties I wondered if I might be the first Englishman to write Irish poetry. This is the fourth poem in my jazz quartet:

97

> In hotel rooms, in digs you went to school.
> These dead were voices from the floor below
> Who filled like an empty room your skull,
>
> Who shared your perpetual one-night stand
> – The havoc there, and the manoeuvrings! –
> Each coloured hero with his instrument.
>
> You were bound with one original theme
> To compose in your head your terminus,
> Or to improvise with the best of them
>
> That parabola from blues to barrelhouse.

Atlantic Records closed years ago. (Solly Lipsitz who prescribed all those new records with an almost medical precision, remains one of my closest friends.) I now buy early jazz on CDs. Computer-enhanced and digitally remastered, seventy-year-old recordings sound as fresh as yesterday. Though my chief enthusiasm continues to be the jazz of the Twenties and Thirties, I recently fell in love with the quirky melodic lines of Thelonius Monk, one of the original boppers ("The music Pythagorian, / one note at a time / Connecting the heavenly spheres," to quote the American poet Charles Simic.) And I have been reaching back to the beginning of the century and transcriptions from piano rolls of compositions by Scott Joplin and other ragtime composers. Jazz is huge. That the suffering and degradation of slavery should bring forth so much redemptive beauty is miraculous. The spontaneity of this music must be one of the best antidotes against authoritarian systems that would tell us what to think and how to feel. Its emergence in the century of the jackboot is of the greatest cultural importance. Stalin hated it. The Nazis hated it. They were frightened of swing. Syncopation is the opposite of the goose-step. Perhaps jazz is our century's most significant contribution to the culture of the world.

Le Symbole
collagraph
JEAN DUNCAN

from HOPEWELL HAIKU

PAUL MULDOON

LIV

An airplane, alas,
is more likely than thunder
to trouble your glass.

LV

On the highest rung
of my two-pointed ladder
a splash of bird-dung.

LVI

Immediately you
tap that old bell of millet
it somehow rings true.

LVII

While from the thistles
that attend our middle age
a goldfinch whistles.

LVIII

A small, hard pear falls
and hits the deck with a thud.
Ripeness is not all.

LIX
Wonder of wonders.
The plow that stood in the hay's
itself plowed under.

LX
Take off his halter
and a horse will genuflect
at a horse-altar.

LXI
Bivouac. Billet.
The moon a waning of lard
on a hot skillet.

LXII
For I wrote this page
by the spasm ... The spasm ...
A firefly ... A cage.

ULSTER AND AMERICA
A Visual Correspondence

LEE WRIGHT

When the cosiness of the mantelpiece is transposed into the New York skyline it becomes clear that symbols of a nation - the carriage clock, the flower girl, have a complexity of meanings which

Plus £15 Leisure Voucher with every new policy

NEW YORK, NEW YORK

Take out a Home Contents Insurance policy now and you could win the holiday of a lifetime to New York

Home Contents - Your peace of mind is our policy

Advertisement for Abbey National Building Society 1997

can be transferred to icons of American-ness. The familial relationship between the Old World and the New World is being visualised and for Ulster this is a pertinent relationship.

The history of emigration from Ireland to North America plays a large part in the heritage culture of Ulster to the extent that the 'Ulster -American Folk Park' is dedicated to it; the literature describes it as, 'An outdoor museum which tells the story of emigration in the eighteenth and nineteenth centuries.'[1] However the logo of the wagon train tells a story of an internal geographical relocation of peoples,

Ulster-American Folk Park entrance 1997

rather than the trans-atlantic journey. One must assume that the perceived notion of 'a journey', and in particular, an American one, is so strongly represented by the nineteenth-century carriage that it encapsulates the museum's intent and ethos. Perhaps this is an example of the potency of Hollywood westerns where the imagery constructed for us through film becomes our reference points of historical knowledge.

This essay selects a variety of images and objects from Ulster which provide us with different ways of visualising America. And it is the corporate symbols and trademarks of U.S. products which are most in evidence among our material culture. The transatlantic connection between two of the Ulster-based textile companies – Fruit of the

Loom[2] and Lee jeans – is not just in the products being available but based on a manufacturing and economic link. This has embedded itself into the local communities and in doing so reinforces the Atlantic connection. At first sight the two corporate identities appear dissimilar. The hand drawn illustrative style of the fruit symbolises a homeliness and equates textile production with the products of nature.

105

A naturalness of the process and ultimately the product is being emphasised. Meanwhile the jeans signage proclaims a social and economic triumph.

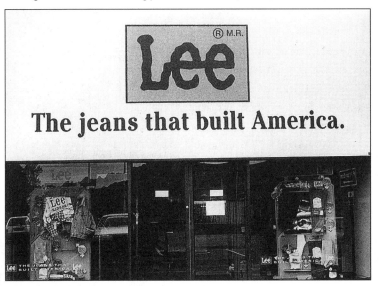

Fruit of the Loom logo

These images demonstrate the two sides of the American Dream. Product labels of Fruit of the Loom state 'Styled in the U.S.A. a product of integrity, established in 1851' while the slogan 'the jeans that built America' recalls a pioneering spirit as the foundation of a modern nation. By 'branding' these products on their (and the nation's)

Frontage of the Lee manufacturing plant in Newtownards, 1997

historical past, an identity has been secured. To a country founded on emigration, identity is, according to writer Robert Hughes, of huge importance. In his most recent book, *American Visions*, he comments:

106

> A culture raised on immigration cannot escape feelings of alien-ness,and must transcend them in two possible ways: by concentration of 'identity', origins and the past, or by faith in newness as a value in itself.[3]

In my opinion the two logos link an industrial history with a moral one and this typifies ways in which America is perceived.One of the most enduring and reproduced paintings of early nineteenth – century America is by Edward Hicks, titled 'Peaceable Kingdom'.[4] A nation in the process of formation is not represented by its industrial progress but by its social acceptance of cultural diversity within a moral and utopian framework. The loyalty of consumer response via purchase of these products also 'buys into' the ethos the products represent. It is from this emotional connection under-scored by branding that a sense of identity emerges, as to what is American and what it stands for. For example, the egg yolk yellow of the golden-arched 'M' of Macdonald's[5], the uniquely moulded proportions of the Barbie Doll or the figurative script and bottle of Coca Cola are legends of object and image making in the history of design. In fact one author comments that Coke is the 'sublimated essence of all that America stands for.'[6]

Wendy's Restaurant, Belfast 1997

So are the most well-known objects in charge of creating our understanding of America and its national characteristics simply because they are the most prolific within our cultural horizon? The answer has to be, in some ways, yes! Not only is the item positioned in every major retail outlet but the process of global marketing has been made most effective by the U.S.A.

107

> To the American manufacturer, the mass market is what mattered; paramount were the convenience and buying habits of the many and not the few.[7]

The system or process of global marketing relies on standardisation[8] and consumer reliance that the item they know in one town or country is the same everywhere else. The Americans broke down the global frontier not by making their products 'fit in' to the culture they were marketed in, but by retaining their original form. Therefore they are able to capitalize and sell American-ness simultaneously. But as I mentioned before, the image is selective and often exploits the era when the American Dream was at its closest to fulfilment – the 1950's. This is echoed in the packaging of some of the most recent Americana to enter Ulster. The imagery of the Wendy's restaurant bag reminds us that the

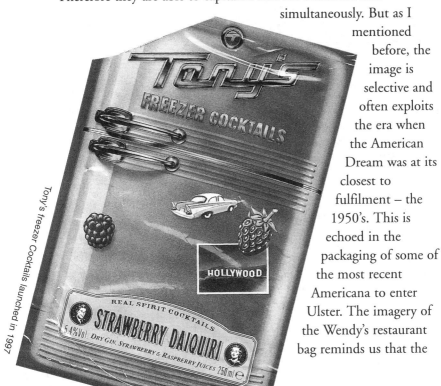

Tony's freezer Cocktails launched in 1997

conquest of the space frontier was American but the illustration is not 1990's technology but a cruder representation which alludes to comics and 1950's science fiction. So too the new Freezer Cocktails wrapped in cadillac pink foil emulate the streamlined refrigerators of the American post war period. Collectively a picture is built up of glamour and assertion because it is the DIFFERENCE to a European visual aesthetic which makes it unique and therefore distinct.

Promotional flyer for Domino's Pizza, Lisburn Road, Belfast 1998

These packages are reminders of a bygone age which we are probably most familiar with through television programmes such as 'Happy Days', and other media sources. So our understanding of American culture is connected to a complex referencing system through other products and the media constructions. The style of the pizza advert recreates one of the most renowned illustrators of the twentieth century, Norman Rockwell.[9]

The preponderance of American products in our consumer experience may be relatively small but often they are on a large scale or so repetitive, (Dunkin' Donuts and the Holiday Inn, for example) that imitation and mimicry occur. Anthony Smith calls it 'a pastiche of cultural motifs and styles'.[10] This is not America referencing its own culture but our culture regurgitating American ideas. A fascinating contemporary example is Virgin Cola which took the classic 'dynamic curve' of the Coke bottle and refigured it into 'The Pammy' (a reference to Pamela Anderson of *Baywatch*). The debate as to the femininity of the Coke classic[11] was instantly superseded by a more curvy example where the meaning was not ambiguous as the name was printed on the bottle. Updated into the 'Wild Pammy' in late 1997, such imagery does not deflect from the American-ness but encourages it by making a visual pun. Even the Pammy Drinks dispenser pastiches a classic of American Art by reproducing a Pop Art theme of Andy Warhol.

The limited edition 'Wild Pammy' issued October 1997

Coca Cola bottle 1998

The Virgin Cola Dispenser, Virgin Cinema Belfast 1998

The Spar sign designed
by Raymond Loewy
Consultants USA

110

The Texaco logo

All these accumulate to
BRAND an American ethos,
an idea so strong that many
American designed logos use
the idea of 'stamping an
identity' based on the concept
of the branding iron.

If many of the examples I have selected can be categorised as essentially urban or drawing on urban culture from the nineteenth century onwards, there is another realm of imagery less obviously attributable . It is perhaps best categorised as concerning the rural and folk traditions which have arisen as vernacular styles pertinent to particular regions. These contrast greatly with the national icons as they are not global classics of highly visible material culture but largely invisible as signatures of America. They symbolize the OTHER AMERICA defined by the image of the picturesque, of which a good example is The American Garden at Florence Court in Co Fermanagh, which 'largely retains its original form'.[12] Created in the mid-nineteenth century as a result of a visit to north America, the notion of a plantation of North American tree and plant specimens, though not uncommon, was considered to be exotic.[13]

An interest in the rustic is definitely part of the Ulster visual experience, possibly for a number of reasons. Linking back to my

111

The American garden in 1875. Still virtually the same today
at Florence Court, Enniskillen

initial comments on the familial relationships and the history of emigration, it would seem to be a more likely transference as families holiday in local areas and regions rather than more typical destinations.

Also there is a strong Irish tradition of the picturesque[14] just as there is in American art and literature. The garden furniture of Al Fresco Designs, Portstewart, faithfully reproduces the 'Adirondack Chair', a design which, although it emanates throughout America, belongs typically to the East coast, and reflects a small geographic regional style of upstate New York. Cumbersome with a rustic charm, this lawnfurniture is suited to adequate sized gardens and therefore may appeal to an Ulster rural heritage where land population is sparse.[15]

Produced by John McGrath of Al Fresco Designs, Portstewart

Housing development near Newtownards, County Down 1997

Similarly, the rusticity of a 'uniquely American style', the Shingle style, is utilised but this time as an influence and inspiration rather than imitation. The 'Teal Rocks' housing development on the shores of Strangford Lough uses local materials and a folk style of architecture (log cabin) to create a home in sympathy with the enviroment. The emphasis is on the natural.[16]

These rustic examples are and have been 'inventing a tradition' for Ulster, a definition which Hobsbawm elucidates as an attempt 'to establish continuity with a suitable historic past'.[17] What is interesting is the selection which is in evidence around us which in some way is considered 'appropriate form' and therefore has been 'appropriated'! If many of the earlier examples are obvious because they stand out, then there are as many which are largely invisible because they blend in. Naturalism is a legacy of the picturesque and Bermingham characterises this as '... roughness, irregularity, fragmentation, the focus on objects and their expressive opportunities'.[18.] They contradict the homogenous aesthetic of 'branded America'.[19] The visual appeal is connected to a craft aesthetic of a more organic style, one which expresses its rusticity rather than offer a machined and standardized

product. These items do not express American idealism in quite the same way as Levis jeans for example, as they do not represent the 'corporate' (or national) view because they illustrate the regional or parochial: 'If there is a traditional American aesthetic, it has evolved through commerce, not art' is a dominant viewpoint[20] because we choose to perceive America as a national homogenous domain which the products with those characteristics echo. Nathaniel Owings defies many authors including Susan Marling who wrote *American Affair: The Americanization of Britain*[21] by saying it is the landscape of RURAL America where their 'national substance lies'.[22]

113

In my view these Ulster designs may reflect the conservative values of localised America (and therefore more accurately the American way) but tell us most about the symbiotic relationship between the two. The integration demonstrates a level of acceptance of values and ethos of meaningful distinction which the imperialistic product with no adaptation to local conditions does not.[23]

ENDNOTES

1 Taken from the promotional Visitor Map and Guide. Ulster-American Folk Park, Castletown, Omagh, Co. Tyrone.

2 The first factory opened in Derry in 1991. The company is the largest under wear manufacturer in the U.S.A.

3 Hughes, R. *American Visions* (London, Harvill), 1997, p. 4.

4 See Hicks (1780-1849) 'Peaceable Kingdom' 1834. National Gallery of Art, Washington,D.C. Reproduced in Hughes, *American Visions*, p.2.

5 Macdonald opened in the USA in 1955. Northern Ireland was 'Donaldized' in 1991,the first one opened in Belfast. See the Business News section of the *Belfast Telegraph* April 8th 1997. It is the largest restaurant chain in the world. (*The Times* London 21/1/95)

6 Pendergast, M. *For God, Country and Coca Cola* (London, Wiedenfield, 1993), p 198.

7 Woodruff, W., *America's Impact on the World.* (London, MacMillan,1975), p. 110.

8 See Houshell, D. *From the American System to Mass Production* (London, John Hopkins, 1994).

9 Buechner, T.S., *Norman Rockwell, a Sixty Year Retrospective* (N.Y. Harry Abrahams Inc., 1972). This book demonstrates clearly the Rockwell 'style'.

10 See Smith, A. D. 'Towards a Global Culture?' in Featherstone, M., *Global Culture* (London, Sage, 1990), p. 176.

11 See Oliver, T., *The Real Coke The Real Story,* (London, Elmtree, 1986).The curvy prototype was developed in 1915.

12 Later renamed the Pleasure Grounds. See National Trust Publication on Florence Court 1992, but a more detailed though unpublished survey by Terence Reeves Smyth was commissioned in 1987 (available in Florence Court archives). This includes a detailed plant specification.

13 See Malins, E., *Lost Demesnes – Irish Landscape Gardening* (London, Barrie and Jenkins, 1976).

14 See Hussey, C., *The Picturesque* (London, Frank Cass, 1967) and Mordaunt Crook, J., *The Dilemma of Style* (London, Murray, 1987).

15 The definitive book on the regional style of the Adirondacks is Gilborn, C., *Adirondack Furniture and the Rustic Tradition* (New York, Abrahms, 1987), p. 279.

16 A detailed study of the style is found in Scully, V., *The Shingle Style* (London, Yale, 1974).

17 Hobsbawn, E., *The Invention of Tradition* (London, Cambridge, 1992), pp. 1 to 13 are the most useful.

18   Bermingham, A., *Landscape and Ideology* (London, Thames and Hudson, 1987), p. 114.

19   See Southgate, P., *Total Branding By Design* (London, Kegan Paul, 1994). Useful for a contemporary discussion of this concept.

20   Owings, N., *The American Aesthetic* (New York, Harpers and Row, 1967), p. 16.

21   Marling, S., *American Affair – The Americanisation of Britain* (London, Boxtree, 1986).

22   Ibid., p. 150.

23   Lorenz, C., *The Design Dimension* (London, Blackwell, 1986).

Thy Self
screenprint
EDDIE GRIGSBY

WAX

JENNIE CORNELL

Barry Kincaid could hypnotise anyone, and he didn't need crystals, or a gold watch and chain. He'd been a child in Draperston when a traveling showman so entranced a local woman that she sat on display in a shop window for fifty-two hours, before Barry stepped forward and broke the spell. At seventeen he'd cured a woman with a riot of symptoms who had labeled the painful parts of her body with the names of the medical men and women who had treated her previously, without success. His most famous case was that of a man who'd not crossed a road in sixty-four years; even a few of the English papers had printed a photo of the man and Barry, walking together through an open field.

Signs led us through the hotel lobby and up the stairs to the second floor till we reached a long table trimmed with posters of Barry. Behind the table sat two girls with clipboards. Symptoms? one of them asked my father, while the other one counted our money and recorded the sum before pulling two tickets from the deck in her hand. My father described how he had trouble sleeping, how he'd tried requesting additional hours in the hope that exhaustion would help him rest undisturbed, but with orders away down and nothing new coming in, he'd been cut back to three days a week instead. At home he'd start books he wouldn't finish and cook us large meals he barely touched. Though by now I'd begun to accept that apart from keeping a blanket ready there was little I could do, the first time it happened I panicked: I snapped my fingers and waved my hands, called his name loudly, even shook his arm though the doctor I'd rung had advised against it, but he never noticed. For over an hour we'd stood together in the open doorway, until my father turned without warning and went back up to

bed of his own accord.

Stress, maybe? the first girl offered, consulting a list of available options.

You tell me, my father answered. The girl stopped her pencil just short of the page and eyed him without humour. Aye, alright, he added dryly. That'll do.

We were put into groups according to malady. There were seven each of smokers and addicts, nine overeaters and six who drank too much. Those with arthritis went in early while a party of people suffering from migraine were still checking in with the cloakroom attendant in the lobby downstairs. Bed-wetters and nail-biters went in with their parents just as the pregnant women came out, talking of buckets of cold and hot water, induced anesthesia, and quick, painless birth. The lone individual with constipation emerged with a look of relief on his face. In fact, only those troubled by low self-esteem or a lack of self confidence reappeared looking much the same as before.

One of the men in our group had a dog with him the size of a hen. When they called us in finally the dog hurried after him, but the man at the entrance collecting tickets halted the queue and reached back to seize the other man's sleeve.

Hold on, mate, he said. You can't bring him in there.

The other man shrugged. What can I do? He won't leave me alone. I put up fences and he digs out under them. He jumps out the windows if he's locked in the house. He's like bloody Houdini. I've tried to get rid of him, but he won't stay away.

I don't make the rules, the ticket man told him. But he's not gettin' in.

Again the man shrugged. I've given up, he answered. If you think you can stop him, go right ahead.

Just grab'm for us, will youse? said the ticket man wearily, so the man caught the dog by its scruff and handed it over while someone else fetched a bin; it took all three to get the dog underneath it, and even then I was sure it would soon claw its way out. He'll be alright, the ticket man told us crossly as we filed past him. You got a problem, ring

the USPCA.

Though he'd led the way into the auditorium, my father left the choice of seating to me. From what remained I selected a place near the front well away from the exits, but still I disliked the distance between us enforced by the wide, outstretched arms of our chairs, so I got up from mine and stood next to my father's.

Now don't start, luv, he said. Go on, now, sit down. I'm here, amn't I? I won't run away.

I knew he wouldn't. He was a man who honoured commitments, and I'd made him promise he'd attend in good faith. All the same, it hadn't been easy. If his condition was worsening, as everyone said, it was largely because he'd relinquished concern for it and no longer bothered to fill prescriptions or show up when scheduled for further tests. At my insistence he had seen a specialist, but two days later he was halfway to Poleglass in his nightshirt and slippers, with no explanation whatsoever to offer the occupants of the RUC landrover which had been his escort for nearly a mile. They brought him home discreetly enough, but still the curious had come to their windows and rumours began that the two were related, my mother's absence and his arrest. Only then would he look at the clippings I'd saved, praising Barry. Why not, eh? he said finally, after weeks of resistance, There's no reason not to. It can't do any harm.

What time d'you have, luv? my father asked the woman beside him. When she told him he grunted and turned away.

He's worth the wait, the woman assured him. I've come eight times now and I always enjoy it.

My father cast me a look of gloomy triumph. Where have you brought me, wee girl, he muttered. Eight times, for God's sake, and he's not cured her yet?

Yet when Barry did step from behind the curtain onto the stage my father sat up and straightened himself like a schoolboy. To save time he'd lost in earlier sessions, Barry dispensed with his introduction and instead moved at once to what he predicted was our most likely fear: that he would abuse his power over us to entertain others, knowing hypnosis could provide us no cure. While it was true, he admitted, that the treatment worked only when we did not resist it, even so he could make us do nothing that would cause us embarrassment, or was opposed in any way to our moral sense – nothing, in short, that we'd not freely agree to when conscious and in full control. The ordeal would be painless, he promised, and there was no chance that having gone under we would not wake up. The rest was a question of self-empowerment, and our own willingness to abandon ideas that had no foundation, no matter how fiercely we might believe them.

Are youse ready? he asked with sudden energy, and the whole room nodded. When he gave the signal we placed our right elbows on the arms of our chairs and, as instructed, thought about things that weren't in the room while he spoke quietly to our open palms – Fingers, rise up now, he was saying, Muscles, contract – until I saw arms everwhere lift off their cushions, and thought about Gulliver waking from slumber, how even the locks of his hair were secured. Once, as part of a cross-community venture, I'd attended a service at which Catholics and Protestants had gathered together to share their experience of a common God. When they bent their heads to enter a prayer I too closed my eyes and folded my hands and opened my heart to the same Holy Spirit I could sense communing with the others there, but still I remained outside the experience, alone among the genuine many whose faith in each other and in Heaven was as palpable as steam. Now the same failure opened my eyes to the faces around me whose expressions were as I knew mine had been: pinched with the effort of concentration, distracted by appetite, incomplete conversations, worrisome footsteps in the room overhead – the difference being, however, that unlike me, they'd refused to give in. The previous year I'd had a teacher who had read aloud from Virgil's *Aeneid* while a bat induced chaos all over the room. Its evasive arcs and sudden diagonals had produced such hysteria that another instructor from a classroom next-door had stepped in finally to protest the noise, and even then he'd kept on reading. Only when the caretaker arrived with a broom and murdered the beast did his eyes leave the page. He closed the book then, gathered his things from the desk in front of him and went straight to the headmaster's office, but the next day he was back as if nothing had hap-

pened. Jobs are scarce, luv, my father said when I told him the story. The way things are these days if you give one up you'll not find another. I had no sympathy then for that explanation, siding instead with my mother's argument that the meagre security of the familiar should not be the reason we stay in a place where we're no longer happy. But later, after she'd left us, and the drawers in the kitchen filled up with boxes with a single match in them and the cupboards grew cluttered with weightless tins that rattled when shaken for he would not use the last of anything, and he would not let anyone throw them out—after weeks during which he boiled no water so as not to empty the kettle she'd filled, I began to think it might be more admirable to take on discontent, however sure a contender, if that were the only way left to shield another, to protect someone else from its hammering blows.

When I looked to Barry for the guidance he'd promised I couldn't find him; I didn't realise at first that he'd left the room. Sounding so much like the man himself that no one had noticed when he made the switch, a tape of his voice was slowly winding from one spool to the other in full view of those whose eyes fluttered gently behind their closed lids, their uplifted faces, even my father's, oblivious and serene.

I did not consider stopping the tape, interrupting the session, demanding a refund, at least, if not an apology. Instead I merely stood up and walked out, pulling the door shut on the people behind me just as Barry emerged from a lift on the far side of the hall.

Hullo, he said. What're you out here for?

His expression was that of a man called away from enjoying a short-lived pleasure to attend to a matter which any number of others could have handled as well as he. I shook my head dumbly.

Who is it you're with? The big fella, isn't it? Is that your daddy?

I nodded. We looked at each other in silence for a moment, then he thrust his hand in his pocket and rattled his change.

I'm not a magician, he said, as if refuting an accusation. There's only so much a person can do.

I didn't deny it. I'd tried everything with my father and it had made no difference.

How old are you ? he demanded abruptly, then complained, when I told him, that I didn't look twelve. I began to explain I was tall for my age when he said just as suddenly, Give us your hand—and keep those eyes closed, too, till I tell you to open them. An awkward movement tugged me towards him and again I heard the tinkle of coins. I'm going to give you a penny, he continued, adjusting his grip, and I want you to close your fist over it; tight, now; that's it. Now don't let go of it till I give you the signal.

I felt the hot press of that coin, could feel its two faces imprinting my skin, and thought yet again of opportunities I'd wasted, knowing at once I'd miss this one, too. On a school trip to Paris with Protestant children I'd seen an American carve her name into the Arc d'Triumph. She'd been with two others who'd watched her do it and held her things for her while she gouged at the stone. I'd wanted at least to register protest, but a boy I fancied had threatened to leave me, to pretend not to know me if I made a scene. I'd done nothing either the time I'd been a witness in the company of others headed up Botanic Avenue towards University Street – middle-aged men in professional attire, bakery girls in their pinnies and caps, a gaggle of students whose jackets and cardigans, too warm for the season, were tied round their waists, and a boy with long hair directly in front of me, a large, lazy dog on a lead by his side – all ambling past a man who wore boots that had seen lots of action, lounging with three others like him on the broken front step of a derelict house. He'd pushed off from the wall with the unhurried thrust of a swimmer reversing, and then kicked the boy's dog so hard its ribs cracked. The boy clutched the lead close to the collar, crossed the street at a trot and hurried back towards Donegal Pass while the animal screamed and I kept on walking, we all kept on walking, past the uniformed guard at the gate to the Gardens, past the RUC vehicle parked just inside, and there was no reason for it, we would have risked nothing, no one need ever have known we'd informed.

You can open your eyes now, Barry said finally, then he placed his hands on my shoulders as I stood in front of him, blocking the way, and not ungently moved me aside. Keep the penny, he added lightly—

a wee souvenir, so you don't forget me. Of course, he continued, if you don't want to keep it, you could give it back.

My eyes fell to my palm and its contents, still tightly scrolled, but like other watched things it remained unresponsive though I used all my strength to will its release. Yours it is, then, Barry said. Then he slipped back into the room behind me, and I heard the door just brush the carpet, twice, like a breath. Across the hallway the lift split open and a cleaner appeared, wheeling a barrow whose stock of towels wobbled deliciously, the mischievous spring of the laundered fabric barely containable under her hand. Won't be long now, luv, she called when she saw me. They'll be comin out t' there any minute, you'll see.

Days seemed to pass, though the clocks didn't show it. Then at last the door fell away from my back and my father appeared with a boy whose arms were thin above the elbow and whose cheeks and chin looked unused to razors.

You'll do it, then? I heard the boy say while the room emptied like an egg around us. You promise?

Right away, my father answered.

Thanks a lot, the boy said earnestly, and gave my father a set of keys. We crossed the courtyard together to the security gates and stepped out onto the street, where taxis had queued to collect the departing. The boy looked both ways as though expecting an ambush, then took off at a run away from the town.

What did he want? I asked my father.

Just a wee favour, luv. He doesn't have time to do it himself.

The boy was a joyrider who'd ignored several warnings. When he was finally forced out of Twinbrook, he'd had every intention of keeping the promise extracted from him to give up the habit and settle down, but after three months the boredom had got to him. He'd stolen a Jetta and driven clear to Lough Swilly, where, on an impulse, he drove the car in. He slammed his foot down as it entered the water and hung onto the wheel, casting a broad plume of surf in his wake like a cheer. He'd done the same with a Clio, an Audi, a couple of Escorts, amused,

for a while, by feigning sympathy when the thefts were discussed the following day. This time, however, he'd heard they were on to him. A friend of his mother's, whose own son had been kneecapped, had told her this time they'd shoot him dead, but still his mother had gone to appeal. Because of her he'd been granted twenty-four hours to get out of the country. He was catching the ferry to Scotland that night.

But what's he want you for?

He keeps bees, my father explained, as if the incredibility of it still made some part of him widen with awe. He's got a hive on the roof of Unity Flats.

I'd walked through there once, out of necessity, detoured by partitions the police had erected to block out the sight of a Loyalist protest marching down from the Shankill to the City Hall. Processions were coming from many directions, and there had been fearful talk of the consequences if those with opposing aspirations were to spot each other along the way. Inside the complex the concrete facades had towered above me and I'd had the impression of walls caving in. The Executive was tearing it down now, however, and erecting two- and three-bedroom houses in its place; only a few of the original buildings were still inhabited. Most of the curtains had been pulled from their windows, the naked panes torn by objects that left neat holes upon entry, as if the glass had been soft and silent when it broke. Disused balconies on the lower floors were filling with rubbish from passing pedestrians, and the stairwells had the fugitive look of abandoned campsites. Even the murals were outdated now and beginning to fade.

On the roof of the building the boy had specified sat the hive, raised on cinder blocks and facing south, near a faucet that swelled and dripped and a hut containing the boy's tools and brushes. On a nail by the hut hung a muslin jumpsuit which my father ignored. He'd been stung so often he could approach any colony, managed or wild, without protection, even open a hive ungloved and bare-chested while their bright, humming bodies settled on his. I hadn't his courage. An acquaintance of his, having heard of his talent, asked him once to dispose of a nest he'd found in a tree on his property, from which large

numbers of bees set out each day. When I joined my father on that inspection I insisted the insects be well sedated before I drew close. Now, squatting comfortably to one side of the hive, he called me over.

It' s alright, he insisted when I shook my head. C'mere till you see.

The boy had told him that the queen might be failing and that he suspected the colony was preparing to swarm. I watched from a distance as they whirred and huddled, trying to summon what I knew about bees—that through an intricate, mathematical language they communicate distance and direction, and yet are myopic, confused by the movement of branches and leaves; that the queen bee, once mated, returns to the hive and never leaves it; that some fifty thousand of her children, working together, perform the life functions of a single being, the survival of each depending on all. My father and I had begun reading books about their behaviour during the twenty-eight months he worked for a farmer transporting honey and beeswax candles to health food groceries throughout the North. The farmer, whose business was small but successful, had approved of my father's undesigning enthusiasm and enlisted his help in the run up to harvest. But then the man's son was murdered in Derry and he sold the business. He sold his house, too, and moved to New Zealand, and my father, who could not afford to buy it from him, was forced to give up the van he'd been driving and find work in a factory, away from bees.

With no trees nearby for the swarm to land on, the boy had provided a short wooden scaffold in a bucket of sand. A few scouts moved busily along its crossed beams, relaying their signal to the rest of the colony; already a slender column had struck out from the hive. Leave her, my father said when one of their number stopped on my sleeve, arguing furiously with the threads that delayed her before flying on. Of the short films on nature we'd been shown in school recently, the best was a slow-motion sequence which revealed the demanding contortions that various species of flight involve. Observing the thickening spout of bodies in motion and wondering how such complex choreographies failed to collide, I almost forgot the unyielding knob of my fist and the coin inside it, out of sight beneath my arm.

Are you tired, luv? my father asked softly. C'mon lean against me. Close your eyes. I'd've been fast asleep myself, to tell you the truth, if it weren't for that wee lad. You should've been there. I reckoned if I didn't talk to him he was going to explode.

126

What is going to happen to him?

He'll be back, my father said simply, then shook his head. I don't know, maybe he won't. God knows I've been wrong before. But don't you despair, luv, he added suddenly. It's not been the worst day. Sure, that story alone was worth the price of admission.

What story?

The one Barry told us when he got back from the loo or the bar or wherever the hell he went to. D'you want to hear it?

I lay back in his arms as he spoke of a woman, blind from birth, whose sight returned soon after she married. When her husband claimed he could draw illness out of the sick like a splinter, the most distinguished of the world's physicians assembled to see him proven a fake. And indeed he was discredited, his entire practice collapsed in disgrace, people who'd spent fortunes to receive the treatment lamented the ease with which they'd been duped—until one of his most tenacious supporters stepped to the front of the amphitheatre and put this question to the crowd: if a man had no better weapon against pain and unhappiness than the medicine of his imagination, would he not still have a marvellous thing? The speaker was heckled, expelled from the professional bodies to which he belonged, later he even broke with his mentor, but no amount of medical evidence could disprove the fact that that woman could see.

At length the flow from the hive abated, and my father released me for a closer look. As the spherical mass at the knot of the cross, shimmering delicately, took to the air, I thought of the perfect rows of hexagonal entries they'd left behind and would build again when they resettled: how good it would be, surrounded by sisters, deep in a place where I fit precisely, where all would defend me if I were threatened, where everything I touched was a part of myself. Then the queen fell

like soot at my father's feet and he knelt with a cry that turned me towards him.

The handful of cohorts that had fallen with her clung to his fingers when he picked her up. He stepped back with his arm upraised and the swarm surged after him like a crowd of revelers who reenter a world where the time is significant to see the last bus of the evening about to depart. When they were first married, friends of my parents acquired a second-hand home movie recorder, which he brought round one evening so they could help him test it out. In that brief film they clasp each other round the waist and shoulders and beam at the camera, their faces pressed close. At the time the house they lived in was empty of furniture apart from a kitchen table and a bed upstairs; in such a space they could waltz or fandango with nothing to hinder them, no obstacle to negotiate or avoid. Now my father moved with the same clean momentum, dipping and spinning, leading the swarm. With the queen imprisoned between his hands, wherever he went he could make them follow.

C'mon, wee woman! he called to me finally, while they churned and swirled round him like a liquid stirred. C'mon, he said. You have a go.

I gave him my wrists and he uncurled my fingers, cupped my hands for me and eased the queen in. I could feel her exploring the crevices there with slow curiosity before the others found her, before my arms were immersed in velvet and cellophane except for the place just above my right elbow where I could still feel my father's sure grip, steering me gently. When we arrived at the edge of the roof, I turned my palms over so they faced the ground, so that anything left there would surely fall out, and then marked their progress until my father, still taller than I then, and with better vision, told me finally that they'd disappeared.

Fine Dining
monoprint/chine collé
GILLIAN THOMSON

HAIKU GATHERING AROUND THE JACKSON BARRACKS PENITENTIARY

RICHARD GODDEN

A cell goes in search
of a cell to fuck. Finds it,
fucks it, and so on …

Just another day
in here, ringed by sharks, circled
by a tornado

Breeze block contradicts
itself, but compared to stone
it is hovering.

Seven black shoes,
somewhere there must be a man
with only one leg.

Linoleum talks
as concrete doesn't; two browns
meet, slow and call out.

Grandfather's stories
put me to sleep, and sank me
into language.

Dull, duller, dullest,
a wall, greyer than grey skies,
is not a window.

130

My lady's gone cold
as cold coffee, and left me
with a blue light on.

Over the forehead,
out through the panoptic eye,
into the locked street.

AH INFINITY!
History is behind you,
run motherfucker.

SYLLABLES. SO YOU
WANT US TO COUNT SYLLABLES.
WHAT ARE SYLLABLES?

—— Dwayne Davis, Richard Godden,
Courtney Huntington, Mary A McCay,
Lawrence Mitchell, Donald Samuels,
Johny Sloan and Dorian Williams.

Invitation
etching
AMANDA JACKSON

THE IRISH SERVANT GIRL IN LITERATURE

MAUREEN MURPHY

The pattern of Irish emigration to the United States is a unique feature of western European migration to America at the end of the nineteenth century. Unlike other nations, Irish emigration was dominated
by single females. The *Report of the Immigration Commission* (1911),
known as the Dillingham Report, found that during the years from
1884-1904, Irish immigrant females outnumbered males for fifteen of
the twenty-two years for which there are records.[1] Although emigration was generally female-dominated, there is less female emigration
literature than male emigration literature. While there are a number of
ballads and songs about young men leaving sweethearts, mothers and
Ireland, there is little that tells about young women's experience. The
Irish immigrant poet Edward Cronin published a ballad, 'The
Maiden's Farewell,' in the Irish-American literary journal *The Gael* that
describes a female, rather than the usual male persona, leaving home
and mother for America:

> But mother! I'm loth sure, to leave you,
> the cottage and the shade boreen
> For I know how my absence will grieve you
> and lonely will be Curraheen.[2]

While the male voices in their emigration poems describe their own
sense of loss leaving Ireland, the maiden of Cronin's poem is concerned
with her mother's rather than her own grief.

Another ballad, 'New Song on the Surprising Victory of an Emigrant
Female over a Desperate Robber and Highwayman who Thought to

Rob Her on her Way to Dublin,' illustrates the spirit and resourcefulness of the Irish emigrant girl.[3] A brave Cavan girl outwits the would-
be robber, shoots him and marries the farmer's son whom she has
impressed with her courage. Then they both go off to America, a sce-
nario that suggests the pair followed her rather than his plans.

Similarly- spirited Irish emigrant girls are the heroines of the ballad
type variously called 'Mary's Lament,' 'Mullinabrone,' 'Philadelphia
Lass' and 'My Bonny Irish Boy' which feature plucky Irish girls who
courageously follows their Wille or Billy to America where their loyalty and ingenuity are rewarded with reunion and marriage.[4] While
young women are capable of bold action, the ballads suggest they feel
their lives are unfulfilled or incomplete without their Irish boys.

American songs about Irish servant girls reflect the anti-Irish
Catholic nativism of the time. An 1863 popular song that exists in several versions opens with the lines:

> I'm a simple Irish girl and I'm looking for a place
> I've felt the grip of Poverty, but sure that's no disgrace
> 'T will be long before I get the one tho' indeed it's hard I try
> For I read in each advertisement, 'No Irish Need Apply.'[5]

Subsequent stanzas point out the irony that the Irish are welcome to
fight for the British Empire and for the Union Army and that the
world admires the work of Irish writers and thrilled to the music of the
Irish soprano Catherine Hayes, but that they are not welcome to work
in this country. The song concludes that a welcome for 'Kathleen'
would demonstrate that America is truly 'the home of Liberty.' Since
versions of the ballad feature a female as well as a male voice, there is
assumption that Irish immigrant women an well as men were literate
and capable of making a clever case for the Irish.

There are also ballads written and sung in Ireland about the returned
Irish immigrant girl. Charles Kickham's popular 'The Irish Peasant
Girl,' better known by its opening lines:

> She lived beside the Anner,
> At the foot of Sliev-na-man,
> A gentle peasant girl,

With mild eyes like the dawn;
Her lips were dewy rose buds;
Her teeth were pearls rare;
A snow-drift 'neath a beechen bough
Her neck and nut-brown hair.[6]

uses the conventions of the traditional aisling or vision poem to describe the idealized beauty of an Irish colleen. Kickham's other work is characterized by his opposition to emigration; his first novel *Sally Cavanaugh* (1869) condemns the evils of landlord abuse and emigration. J.M. Croft's 'Noreen Bawn' ends with the lines:

There's a churchyard in Tír Chonaill,
Where the blossoms sadly wave,
There's a sorrow-stricken mother
weeping o'er that lonely grave,
'Poor Noreen,' she is calling,
"Tis I'm lonesome since you're gone.
"Twas the shame of emigration
Laid you low my Noreen Bawn.'[7]

Both ballads describe beautiful young girls, popular in their own places, gentle and generous, whose health is destroyed by emigration. Kickham's heroine dies in America; Noreen Bawn returns home to Ireland with consumption, the disease of poverty that brought not only death but shame. The phrase 'the shame of emigration' is not only an allusion but the demonstration of the reticence of the Irish to mention tuberculosis by name. The irony of these songs is that the young women who emigrated to better their lives and those of their families went to a worse life than they would have had had they stayed at home.

Courage, resourcefulness and self-sacrifice are the attributes of the Irish emigrant girls in these ballads and songs, and they characterize Irish emigrant girls, particularly the Irish servant girls, in Irish-American fiction. These virtues, particulary self-sacrifice, distinguish the fiction about Irish servant girls from the fiction that focuses on the adventures of Irish immigrant boys who are the heroes of books like: *John O'Brien, or the Orphan of Boston, His Share of the World, The Luck of the Kavanaghs* and *Michael O'Donnell* or the *Fortunes of a Little*

Emigrant. It is no surprise that Horatio Alger created an Irish immigrant boy hero for his rags to riches series. *Only an Irish Boy,* or *Andy Burke's Fortune* follows the Horatio Alger formula: a young man wins his fortune and his happiness through hard work and a test of his moral character.

Irish servant girl fiction is defined by self-sacrifice. Irish male emigrants are expected to succeed; the female is expected to sacrifice: for her parents, her siblings, her extended family, her employer's family and her church. While the servant girl is often rewarded with marriage to a kind, steady man, and sometimes with return to Ireland, it is the survival and prosperity of her family, her father, mother and siblings, that promises her the greatest satisfaction and pleasure.

The virtue of self-sacrifice is reinforced in folklore and mythology. Versions of the international folktale (AT 451), 'The Girl who Seeks her Brothers', were popular in the Irish countryside. In the story, a girl searches for her brothers who have been banished or who have fled because of circumstances associated with her birth. In one version, 'The Twelve Wild Geese,' the brothers disappear because her mother, wishing for a little girl, rashly said, 'I would give away every one of my twelve sons for her.'[8] The girl's quest requires her to be clever and courageous; it also demands self-sacrifice and self-control. In most versions of the story she has to remain silent or pretend that she is dumb even when she is faced with the charge of murder. Bruno Bettleheim observed in *The Uses of Enchantment* that such a story type demonstrates that self-sacrifice makes return to order possible.[9]

Irish mythology has its own example of the self-sacrificing sister in the figure of Fionnuala from *The Fate of the Children of Lir.* Fionnuala confronts her jealous step-mother who cast a spell over the children, transforming them into swans; she explains the terms of their enchantment to her father, and she comforts and shelters her brothers under her own wings during their long exile.

Given the expectations that Irish girls' emigration and employment in domestic service would benefit the family, an expectation reinforced by Irish narrative tradition, it is not surprising to see that self-sacrifice is the *leitmotif* of the Irish servant girl literature. In the nineteenth cen-

tury Irish-American novel she appears first as an incidental character in domestic novels, then as a stereotypical figure and, finally, in her own right as a protagonist.

In his book *The Irish Character in American Fiction 1830-1960*, Stephen Garrett Bolger lists some thirty-five books where an Irish servant girl, usually called Bridget, is a comic figure whose unfamiliarity with American ways provides the humor. In various of the novels Bridget lights a fire on the stove, sips cream from the jug she carries to the dining room and washes a leg of mutton in the hand basin. The literary Bridgets, these nineteenth-century Amelia Bedelias, have their counterparts in the Bridget jokes and cartoons, and, indeed, in the stories that servant girls tell about themselves.

By contrast the Irish servants in the nineteenth-century, Anglo-Irish 'Big House' novels are valuable to their employers precisely because they are able to interpret the native Irish character or culture to the English or Anglo-Irish protagonist. In Maria Edgeworth's novel *Ormond*, when Harry Ormond is horrified by the Black Islanders' passionate grief at King Corney's, Corney's housekeeper Sheelagh Dunshaughlin counsels Ormond:

> Bear with it, Master Harry. Hard for you! – but
> bear with us, dear. 'Tis the custom of the country,
> and what else can we do but what the forefathers did –
> how else for us to show respect, only was it would be
> expected and has always been? [10]

Valuable as their function as interpreters might be, apart from the singular example of *Castle Rackrent's* Thady Quirk, the reader meets servants who are only minor characters, among the cavalcade of country people: tenants, tradesmen, tinkers, prophecymen, paupers, poor scholars, *spailpiní* and schoolmasters who provide local color, never the heroes, for these regional novels. Indeed, when the pony-trader Myles na gCopaleen bursts into Gerald Griffin's *The Collegians* (1829), he threatens to take over and Griffin banishes him. Later, when he adapted the novel for his play *The Colleen Bawn* (1860), Dion Boucicault made Myles the hero of the melodrama. In American domestic novels

137

and on the American stage, the Irish servant girl provided the humor.

Irish servant girls also appeared as stereotypical figures in the sentimental Catholic novels that appeared in the mid-nineteeth century. *John O'Brien or the Orphan of Boston* (1850) and the thinly-disguised tract *The Cross and the Shamrock* or, *How to Defend the Faith, an Irish-Catholic Tale of Real Life Descriptive of the Temptations, Suffering, Trials and Triumphs of the Children of St. Patrick* and the *Great Republic of Washington* (1853), by priests, Fathers John Roddan and Hugh Quigley and John Boyce's (Paul Peppergrass) *Mary Lee or the Yankee in Ireland* (1868) were written to bolster Catholic spirit during the period of the anti-Catholic, anti-immigrant Know-Nothing party. The virtuous servant girl was meant to be a model for her English-literate servant girl reader. They are pious and self-sacrificing (*John O'Brien*); they are courageous in the face of bigotry (*Mary Lee*), and they steadfastly resist the efforts of others, especially employers, who try to proselytize (*Cross and Shamrock*).

At the same time and continuing until the middle of the twentieth century are the Irish-American novels with servant girl heroines. Their pious titles warn the reader that they will not be distinguished for their literary quality: Anna H. Dorsey's *Nora Brady's Vow* (1857), Peter McCorry's (Con O'Leary), *The Lost Rosary* or *Our Irish Girls: Their Trials, Temptations and Triumphs* (1870) and *Mt. Benedict or the Violated Tomb* (1871), John McElgun's *Annie Reilly, or The Fortunes of an Irish Girl in New York: a Tale Founded on Fact* (1878) and Mary Anne Madden Sadlier's *Con O'Regan* or *Immigrant Life in the New World* and *Bessy Conway* (1881).

The Lost Rosary is dedicated to the Irish servant girl herself:

> To the ever faithful Irish girls in America whose affectionate devotion to
> their kith and kin in the old land, has proved that virtue and charity,
> the results of pious and careful training in youth, are unlessened by dis-
> tance and end only with life itself.[11]

David S. Reynolds observed of such novels in *Faith and Fiction: The Emergence of Religious Literature in America*, that 'despite the stress on reason and tradition, Catholic fiction made rhetorical use of sentimental devices which became more prominent as time passed.'[12] While the

novels lack literary quality, they are not without value. They provide descriptions of Irish servant girls' experiences and the contemporary attitiudes toward them, and they demonstrate remarkable verisimilitude. The fictional accounts of the servant girls' experiences reflect the data from servant girls' oral histories and letters and from other information about their experience in America.

While servant girl heroines may emigrate with friends, neighbors or even perhaps siblings, their nuclear families do not re-form in the United States. They emigate to keep their parents and their inheriting brothers on the land. Like most servant girl arrivals to America, Annie Reilly, the heroine of *Annie Reilly* or *The Fortunes of an Irish Girl in New York*, has Mrs. Duffy, a Dublin woman bound for America that she has met on board ship, to see her through her arrival in New York. As she leaves Castle Gardens to meet another friend Kitty Brady, she gives a sympathetic glance to the girls who arrived friendless.

Other servant girls heroines like Mary O'Donnell and her cousin Ailey (*The Lost Rosary*) arrive without a friend to meet them or a place to stay. A beggar woman, a 'runner,' leads them to a disreputable house, but they quickly realize their danger and Ailey sets off to find more suitable quarters. Her method is to pass by a house several times to see whether there are men loitering about the place and then to judge the cleanliness of the place. She notices one house is freshly painted and that there is a picture of the Virgin Mary on the wall. By coincidence, the *sine qua non* of sentimental fiction, the landlady has befriended Mary's beloved Barney McAuley, the young man that the two girls have followed to America.

Servant girls were not only expected to send money home regularly, they were also expected to sponsor their emigrating siblings. When Con O'Regan, hero of *Con O'Regan* or *Emigrant Life in the New World*, thinks of his sister Winny who has paid his passage and found him a job, he speaks of the sacrifices she has made for him:

Ah Winny poor Winny! I'm afeared it's what you left yourself bare and naked to send money home! And I suppose it's often the same story might be told of them that sends home money to Ireland.[13]

The theme of the servant girl novels is the triumph of character, particularly character as informed by Catholic mores. In Sadlier's *Bessy Conway*, when the daughter of a Tipperary farmer emigrates to America, her landlord's son, the profligate Henry Hubert, follows her. Bessy saves and sends money home, and her reward is the immigrant's dream: she returns to Ireland in time to save her family from eviction. Hubert follows her back to Ireland, but he's a reformed man, a Catholic convert inspired by Bessy's example, and Bessy accepts his proposal of marriage. Bessy's friend, Mary Murphy, on the other hand, makes an improvident marriage with Lukey Mulligan. Sadlier uses her favorite device of contrasting good and bad behavior with appropriate rewards and punishments: the loyal, industrious and sensible Bessy Conway who saves her family and marries well versus the flightly Mary Murphy who is given the flashy dressing and going to dances and who makes an unfortunate marriage.

Going home to Ireland and marrying the landlord's son are rewards indeed, but Mrs. Sadlier's sentimental novels reward and punish on a rather lavish scale. More typical is John McElgun's Annie Reilly whose story ends with a suitable marriage to honest and temperate James O'Rourke. Like Bessy, Annie's character brings her safely to marriage through trials to her faith and morals. Such novels were written to warn Irish servant girl readers of occasions of sin: spending money on clothes and going to dances.

The novels fictionalize the kind of advice to Irish emigrant girls given in such books as the Nun of Kenmare's (Margaret Anna Cusack's) *Advice to Irish Girls in America* (1872). It is the sort of counseling that one can find in popular Irish-American literature until well into the twentieth century. As late as 1931, 'Her Evening Out,' a short story that appeared in the Mission of our Lady of the Rosary's monthly magazine *Old Castle Garden*, cautioned Irish servant girls about the danger of going to dances. Misled by the Irish name, Brigit Burke goes to a New York dance hall where she is picked up by a fast talker who offers her drink and tries to take her to Harlem. She is rescued only when they are stopped for speeding, and the story ends with some fatherly advice dispensed by the Irish desk sergeant.

Moralists like Mrs. Sadlier considered dance-going dangerous, warning that it led to drunkeness, to bad marriages or -what was worse- to seduction. Sadlier's Bessy Conway avoids being seduced by Henry Hubert, and Winny O'Regan fends off a pass by the lecherous Dr. Richards. In Sadlier's version of the Potiphar's wife tale, Dr. Richards complains to Winny's mistress that she is insolent and Mrs. Coulter fires her.

While the virtue of the Irish servant girl is seldom compromised, in at least one story, Harvey O'Higgin's 'The Exile' (1906), there is the suggestion that the madness and death of a young Irish servant girl is the result of her seduction and the morbid shame of out of wedlock pregnancy.

Dangerous as it was to an Irish servant girl's morals to be on her own in the city, nineteenth-century servant girl literature was far more concerned with the danger to her faith, and it was a danger to young men as well as to young women. Readers were warned about the danger of missing mass, of befriending Protestants and of public school education. The young men in Sadlier's *Willie Burke* and *The Blakes and the Flanagans* face such temptations. While Peter Burke is saved by his brother's good example, the apostate Blakes suffer hideous punishments: Henry Blake's unbaptized son dies of fits and Eliza Blake, who marries a Protestant, dies in childbirth shrieking for a priest.

All of the Irish servant girl heroines work in Protestant households where their Catholicism is an issue and their faith is tested. They are required to attend family prayers and Bible readings; their household responsibilities interfere with mass, and they are subjected to rude and mocking behavior by other servants or by family members.

Not only do the Irish servant girls pass through their trials with their faith intact, they are among their parishes' most generous benefactors. The author of *John O'Brien or the Orphan of Boston* described that

> excellent specimen of the Boston Irish Catholic young women who do the work in families or otherwise labor hard for their bread. They have done more for the interests of religion in Boston, taking their means into consideration than all other classes put together. They have built St. Mary's Church; they have built every church in Boston. The charity of

the Boston Catholics is proverbial. To be sure, in ages of faith, it would not be regarded as extraordinary, but in these times, it deserves great credit. And these girls have done more than their share of the good work which has given such a name to Catholic Boston. No one has even called upon them in vain. They will often give more than they can afford and their generous hearts make them feel half disposed to apologize for giving so little. And, in truth, a girl of this class often gives actually more to pious purposes than some men who are not poor. She thinks she can afford a dollar. He thinks it's hard times and gives fify cents. The Catholic young woman needs no monuments; their monument is a church in every quarter of the city.[14]

In her defense of her faith, the Irish servant girl draws on her intelligence and her wit. Annie Reilly defends the Catholic position on Bible reading to her mistress, Mrs. Phillips, with an argument that follows the one outlined by the Nun of Kenmare in *Advice to Irish Girls in America*. Winny O'Regan and Mary O'Donnell endure the bigotry of their households, but, like their real-life counterparts, they draw the line at missing mass and proselytism. Eliza Blake's Irish servant girl reports her conversation with Eliza vowing that she will never miss mass:

'I was out at 6:00 mass this morning, thanks be to God, and when I came in it's what she scolded me for going out so early.'
'You'll not be able to keep your eyes open all day,' says she to me, 'and here we are to have the Thompson family to dinner. You should have slept an hour longer, when you were up so late last night.'
'Why ma'am,' says I to her, 'if I didn't get up an' go to six o'clock mass, I couldn't get out at all.'
'Even so,' says she, 'what great harm would it be to miss mass for one day?'
'It would be that much harm, that I wouldn't do it for all you're mistress of. No ma'am! I know I'm a foolish an' light enough in some things, and I'm a poor ignorant girl in the bargain, but I wouldn't miss mass, ma'am for all the money in New York.'[15]

The outspoken independence, lively sense of humor and common sense anticipate the Irish servant girls of twentieth-century American literature and popular culture, figures who were servants but not

servile. Their witty and spirited retorts to their employers became a convention of American domestic literature, and these anecdotes are part of servant girls' oral histories.

In this respect, the Irish servant girl in American literature resembles the parasite/slave character of Roman comedy. They may be awkward country girls, but, with their cheerful self-confidence, they keep the upper hand in their households. Jokes in *The Gael*, an Irish-American periodical of the turn of the century, demonstrate the servant girl's reputation for the sharp retort:

> A lady had in her employ an excellent girl who had one fault. Her face was always in a smudge. Her mistress tried without offending to tell her to wash her face, and at last resorted to strategy.
> 'Do you know, Bridget,' she remarked in a confidential manner, 'it is said that if you wash your face every day with soap and water, it will make you beautiful?'
> 'Will it?' said Bridget. 'Sure, it's a wonder ye never tried it, ma'am.'[16]

Another joke from *The Gael*, titled 'Easily Arranged' is a version of the international folktale motif J 1500, 'The Clever Practical Retort', where a clever answer saves the servant from the master:

> Mistress: 'Now Sarah, you have broken more china in the past quarter than the whole of your wages can cover. What are we to do?'
> Sarah: 'That's more than I can say, ma'am; unless you make ends meet by raising my wages.'[17]

The outspokenness was a measure of the servant girl's confidence. Like George Bernard Shaw's St. Joan, she could say, 'I have dared and dared.'[18] She dared to leave home, to come to America, to work to help her family and to create opportunities for herself, and she negotiated the dangers she met with the force of her character, her intelligence, her wit and her sense of her own self-worth.

In 'Where's Nora?,' one of Sarah Orne Jewett's series of sympathetic stories of Irish immigrants, Nora refuses to go into the Lawrence mills saying she wants to work on the railroad instead. She starts baking and selling cakes and buns on the trains where she meets a nice old gentleman who turns out to be the general manager of the railroad.

143

Impressed by Nora, he offers her the chance to start a station lunch counter. She makes her fortune, marries and takes her son and her old uncle back to visit Kerry. With the expansive gesture of the returned Yank she throws coins to beggars.

144

Mary Ellen McLaughlin, the grandmother in Jack Dumphy's *The Murderous McLaughlins*, has the same sort of spunk. She shouts at her husband, 'Did you expect me to stand still as all of you have? To have learned nothing? To have seen nothing? Not when I crossed the Atlantic.'[19]

According to the immigration historian Oscar Handlin, it was these high spirits as well as cheap wages and especially loyalty that made Irish servant girls welcome in Boston households despite the early 'No Irish Need Apply' nativism.[20] In fiction, it is the servant girl's most admirable and endearing quality. In *Con O'Regan* or *Immigrant Life in the New World*, when Winny O'Regan leaves her own sickbed to care for Rachel Coulter, even the bigoted Mrs. Coulter is moved by Winny's loyalty to the sick child.

Autobiographies and memoirs written by nineteenth- and twentieth-century Americans speak of the same loyalty and affection they experienced from the Irish help in their households. Mark Twain wrote of Katie Leary; Edith Wharton recalled her nurse Hannah Doyle who provided the love she did not receive from her distant mother. The naval historian Samuel Eliot Morrison found his most loving welcome as a boy in the kitchen where the Irish help doted on the little boy.

Harriet Ide Keen Robert's *Nana*, her biography of her Irish nurse's life, demonstrates another kind of loyalty. When her employers the Roberts have financial trouble and there is no money to pay her wages, Nana stays on regardless of whether she receives her wages. Nana has her counterparts in nineteenth century Anglo-Irish fiction : Mrs. Hall's 'The Follower of the Family,' Gerald Griffin's 'The Aylmers of Ballyaylmer.'

Sean O'Faoláin's short story 'The Planet of the Years' demonstrates that the loyalty of the Irish servant girl was not only appreciated, it was reciprocated. The story describes a young Irish woman living in Cambridge where her husband is spending his sabbatical year at

Harvard. One winter afternoon she opens her front door to find two women standing on the steps. The older had come to the house in 1904 as a servant girl. Describing her arrival and her work there over thirty-five years, she said, 'I was contented all day every day as I never was before or since. I found my first and only home in this blessed house.'

The Irish servant girl was not only loyal to her employer family, she often identifed with them. In Mc Sorley's *Our Own Kind*, Ned grumbles about the Flynns who go around bragging about the wealth of their employers and who are admired for working in such households. Such bonds were painfully severed when young charges went off to school and the services of the children's nurse were no longer required. Sondra Spatt Olsen's 'Nursemaid' sympathetically treats the servant girl Nora Donovan who is prevented by her employer from saying good-by to the child she has raised.[21]

The fictional servant girl's identification with the family is complete in Marica Davenport's 1942 best-seller *Valley of Decision*, the chronicle of the Scott family of Pittsburgh from the panic of 1873 to World War II, from the time Mary Rafftery, a 'living out girl,' the daughter of an Irish immigrant, arrives as a maid in the Scott household to Mary at the age of eighty-four. Paul Scott, the son of the family, loves Mary, but she refuses to marry him because the differences in class would mean that Paul would be forced to give up the family's iron works. In denying her own happiness, Mary saves the family.

Another family son enchanted by his family's Irish servant girls was the essayist John Jay Chapman. Writing about Edmund Spencer and Ireland in a 1924 letter to Emil Legouis, Chapman said:

And by the way, Irish young women are not only the handsomest, and the most maddeningly beautiful and womanly girls in the world but the most romantic, mysteriously religious and unearthly. We had for two years a cook and a maid — sisters, young, small and red haired - not especially beautiful — but good-looking — elfin beings, dreamland beings, very Catholic, very quiet very chaste. Everytime I met one of them stepping demurely upstairs I felt as if smitten with a wand. I suspect there's a good deal of Ireland in Spencer's *Faerie Queene*.[22]

145

We know that much mythology descends to folklore. In Irish folk-lore, Saint Brigit is often described as a servant girl or as performing servant girl duties. The name itself is associated with servant girls so much so that the *Oxford English Dictionary* defines Biddy as '... the familiar abbreviation for Bridget used chiefly in the United States for an Irish maid or servant.' Irish servant girls recall they were often addressed not by their own names but as Biddy or Bridget. The name was institutionalized at Harvard to describe the women who looked after generations of undergraduates.

It is an appropriate connection because it is the example of St. Bridget, perhaps as much as anything, that reinforces the image of the selfless Irish servant girl not only as she appeared in Irish-American fiction but, what is more important, as she appeared to herself.

ENDNOTES

1. United States Immigration Commission, *Abstract of Reports of the Immigration Commission*, I (Washington: Government Printing Office, 1911), Table 9: Immigration to the United States, 1820 - 1910, Part 2: By Country of Origin and by Sex for the Years ending June 30, 1869 to 1910, pp.87 – 95.
2. Edward Cronin, 'The Maiden's Farewell', *The Gael* (April 1900) 119. There is a townland called Curraheen in Cronin's native Limerick.
3. 'New Song on the Surprising Victory of an Emigrant Female over a Desperate Robber and Highwayman who thought to Rob her on her Way to Dublin', *Irish Emigrant Ballads and Songs* ed. Robert L. Wright (Bowling Green: Bowling Green University Popular Press, 1975), pp.100 -101.
4 'Mary's Lament', 'Mullinabrone', 'Philadelphia Lass', 'My Bonny Irish Boy', Ibid., pp.391, 392, 394, 397 – 9.
5 'No Irish Need Apply', Ibid., pp. 650–652. The sheet music for this song was published by S. Brainerd in 1863; there is a copy in the Library of Congress.
6 Charles J. Kickham, 'The Irish Peasant Girl', *The Dublin Book of Irish Verse*

ed. John Cooke (Dublin: Hodges, Figgis & Co., 1913), pp.415–416.

7. J.M. Croft, 'Noreen Bawn', *Walton's 132 Best Irish Songs and Ballads* (Dublin: Walton's Musical Instrument Galleries, n.d.), p.107.

8 Patrick Kennedy, 'The Twelve Wild Geese', *Irish Fairy and Folk Tales* ed. W.B.Yeats (New York: Modern Library, n.d.), p.300.

9 Bruno Bettelheim, *The Uses of Enchantment* (New York: Vintage, 1977), p.80.

10 Maria Edgeworth, 'Ormond', *Novels and Tales of Maria Edgeworth*, IX (New York: Harper and Brothers, 1850), pp. 148–149.

11 Peter McCorry, *The Lost Rosary* or *Our Irish Girls: Their Trials, Temptations and Triumphs* (Boston: Patrick Donahoe, 1870).

12 David S. Reynolds, *Faith and Fiction: The Emergence of Religious Literature in America* (Cambridge: Harvard University Press, 1981), p. 70.

13 Mary Anne Madden Sadlier, *Con O'Regan* or *Immigrant Life in New York* (New York: Sadlier, 1854), p. 50.

14 John Roddan, *John O'Brien* or *The Orphan of Boston* (Boston: Patrick Donahoe, 1850), p. 206.

15. Mary Anne Madden Sadlier, *The Blakes and the Flanagans* (New York: Sadlier, 1858), pp. 326 - 327.

16. 'Bridget Was Undoubtedly an Irish Woman', *The Gael*, 19:4 (April 1900), 104.

17. 'Easily Arranged', *The Gael*, 22:7 (July 1903), 139.

18. George Bernard Shaw, *St. Joan* , ed. Stanley Weintraub (New York: Bobs Merrill, 1971), p. 139.

19. Jack Dunphy, *The Murderous McLaughlins* (New York: McGraw Hill, 1988), p. 49.

20. Oscar Handlin, *Boston's Immigrants* (New York: Atheneum, 1969), p. 61.

21. Sondra Spatt Olsen, 'Nursemaid', *The Gael*, 11:1 (Winter 1983), pp. 12–14.

22. M.A. DeWolfe Howe, *John Jay Chapman and His Letters* (Boston: Houghton Mifflin, 1937), p. 401. I thank Professor Joann Krieg for bringing this letter to my attention.

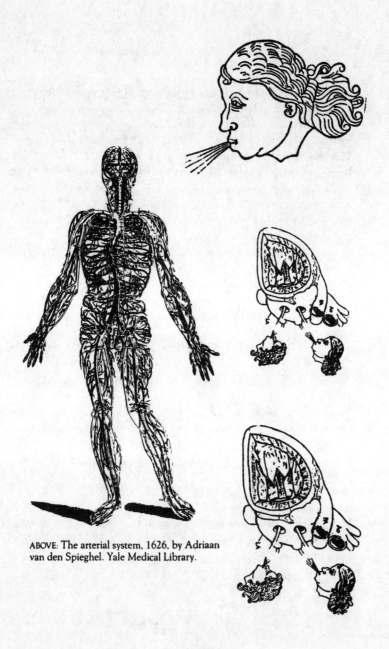

ABOVE: The arterial system, 1626, by Adriaan
van den Spieghel. Yale Medical Library.

Breath of Life
lithograph
BECKWITH THOMPSON
TEXAS TECH UNIVERSITY

EVOLVING REPRESENTATIONS OF REPUBLICAN WOMEN:
Northern Ireland and the Socio-Politics of British Television Drama

JENNIFER C. CORNELL

INTRODUCTION

Most teleplays concerned with the violence in Northern Ireland and produced in the United Kingdom prior to the 1985 signing of the Anglo-Irish Agreement reflect the policy of 'criminalisation' which defined the British Government's official response to Irish Republicanism during most of Margaret Thatcher's regime. In keeping with this policy, the perpetrators of violence depicted in the teleplays of this period tend to fall into one of two categories: those who can and should be held responsible for their actions, and those who can not, by reason of psychological imbalance, emotional immaturity, or political naïveté.

Though there are exceptions, perpetrators of the first type were and remain predominantly male. Most often depicted as psychopaths, deviants, or fanatics, these men are characterised by the premeditation of their violence, its ferocity, and by their own utter lack of remorse, underscored by other elements of the visual narrative such as soundtrack, cinematography, and *mise-en-scene*. Such patterns of representation not only depoliticise the violence portrayed, but make illegitimate the very grievances which are used to explain and justify that violence.

Whatever their politics or ethnicity and whatever the narrative context in which they appear, women are depicted less often as perpetrators of violence than as victims of it, or as advocates of nonviolent, alternative forms of protest. It is not surprising, then, that when they do resort to violence, women have predominated among

those who can not be held responsible for their actions. It is also consistent with popular constructions of the female as the more subjective and emotive sex that the relative innocence of these characters be derived from private weaknesses of their hearts or minds. My purpose in this essay is to trace the representation of Republican women in contemporary British television drama from these simplistic depictions to the more complex portraits which are currently in vogue, and to suggest some reasons for and potential consequences of these changing images for the socio-political future of the Northern Irish state.

A MOON FOR THE MISDIRECTED
Anne Devlin's *The Long March*

As the history of suffrage attests, women's interest in politics has often been downplayed or dismissed as an emotional response to the romantic appeal of a candidate or a cause. In the context of Northern Ireland, such representations not only have perpetuated gender stereotypes, but have contributed to the deliberate misrepresentation of Irish Republicanism as a movement to which only the foolish, unhappy, or directionless are drawn.[1] To illustrate this argument, I offer an analysis of two teleplays by Anne Devlin, both produced for the BBC and first broadcast in 1984.[2]

In *The Long March,* Devlin's protagonist is Helen Walsh. Returning from England to her parents' home in west Belfast following her separation from her husband, Helen arrives at the height of the campaign for special category status by Republican prisoners in 1979. She soon finds work as a researcher with Fergus Sloan, an old friend and former lover who is now a university lecturer. Sloan's recent article on the merits of Republicanism has attracted the attention of a well-known sympathiser, Frank Molloy, whose nephew, Colm, Helen hires as her assistant and community liaison. The drama traces Helen's largely unsuccessful efforts to 'find herself,' first through her job and an affair with Colm, and later by returning to England and to university.

Described by Sloan's wife as yet 'another star-struck protester, living in a never-never land of protest marches and continuous revolution,'

Helen holds beliefs, which, though she feels them keenly, appear to be based on an understanding of the situation in the North which is at best naïve. 'You've been away a long time!' her father retorts when she argues that the Molloys and other supporters of Republican violence are 'still people, ordinary human beings like you and me.' Indeed, despite her friends' and family's obvious distaste for the paramilitaries and their apologists – an antipathy which, unlike her own uninformed enthusiasm, is based on regular, daily contact – Helen remains willfully oblivious, even cavalier, about the consequences for others of her actions and ideas. She hires Colm, for example, without authorization and apparently without thought for the implications of employing a man with Republican sympathies on a project whose success depends on appearing objective. According to those who know her best, such behaviour is typical. 'She's always the same, never thinks of anyone but herself,' her father complains, while her mother observes bitterly that in her youth Helen 'always [walked] away from anything that didn't suit [her],' and ten years later she still hasn't changed.

'I wish you and mummy would stop using the word "failure" about me!' Helen cries during one of her many rows with her father, yet no other word seems quite as apt. Selfish, irresponsible, unable to make a success of her career or her marriage, unable to assimilate in England despite the advantages of wealth and a good education, Helen nurses a nostalgia for the Civil Rights Movement and worries that 'nothing in the present [will] ever [match] up to what was in the past.' It soon becomes clear that all her actions, including her support for the Republican movement, can be explained in terms of a desire to recapture her youth, and the potential and promise of that earlier, more exciting time in her life: her attraction, despite his contempt for her, to the much younger Colm; her abandoned marriage; even her otherwise inexplicable desire to return to the North, which no one who lives there can understand. So determined is she to regain what she's lost, that she's blind to the realities of life in west Belfast. In Andersonstown, for example, where much of the drama takes place, the scenery is dreary, violence commonplace, and practically everyone is unemployed, yet it is here that Helen announces brightly, 'Do you know something? I'm really happy again!'

Because she only plays at politics herself, Helen underestimates the commitment of those around her. Even her ethnicity is all affectation: desperate for a Cause to give her life direction and meaning, she yearns to number among the oppressed, but despite all her efforts she remains an outsider. Colm ridicules her 'fancy accent' and expensive clothes when she claims to come from the Falls, while his friend Mona is openly hostile, remarking suspiciously, 'It's funny, you growing up on the Falls and yet nobody knows you;' later, when Helen tries to reason with her as one Catholic Nationalist to another, Mona rejects her overtures on the same grounds. Even after Helen realises her dream of enrolling in art college, the locals understand her no better. If anything, her new incarnation only estranges her further from the community she had hoped to reclaim as her own.

DEMENTIA, DELINQUENCY, AND INDECENT CRIME:
Anne Devlin's *Naming The Names*

Although her uncritical support for Republicanism puts her friends and family at risk, Helen herself does not participate in any act of violence. Her relative innocence is typical of female characters in the teleplays of this period. Furthermore, of those women whose actions do have fatal consequences, most are only indirectly responsible for the violence they cause. Rather than fire a gun or detonate a bomb themselves, they tend to serve as couriers, decoys, look-outs, and alibis; they are also the bait with which (male) victims are lured to their deaths. This is the role Devlin gives to Finn McQuillen, the protagonist of her other 1984 teleplay for the BBC, *Naming The Names*.

The drama opens with Finn's arrest for complicity in the murder of Henry Kirk, a judge's son with whom she has been having an affair. As she is interrogated, her mind returns to important events in her life, shown to the viewer through flashbacks: her relationship with an English journalist, Jack McHenry; the destruction of Nationalist neighbourhoods in west Belfast by Loyalist mobs; the death of her grandmother; her gradual drift towards Republicanism; and finally, her chance meeting of Kirk, their sudden affair, and her eventual betrayal

of him to the IRA.

In a narrative structured deliberately through flashbacks and dream sequences to disorient the viewer, causal relationships between events are difficult to ascertain. Disentangling Finn's motivations is further complicated by the fact that she suffers from fits and seizures for which no explanation is given, medical or otherwise. She also sleepwalks, is tortured by nightmares, and she hallucinates. Presumably as a consequence of her traumatic childhood, she is alternately depressed and hysterical, and appears to be afflicted with a form of psychosis through which she regresses periodically into the girl she once was. In response to police interrogation she offers what appear to be rational explanations for her actions but which, when juxtaposed with scenes depicting what 'really' happened, are ultimately unconvincing. While her unfortunate history and the eerie beauty of the actress who portrays her make Finn a sympathetic character, nevertheless the effect of these devices is to cast doubt on her reliability as a narrator, and thus to discredit the ideology she claims to espouse.

Significantly, Finn's decision to join the IRA is personal, not political. When a Loyalist mob sets her home alight, she is in a hotel room with McHenry, leaving her elderly grandmother, with whom she lives, to be rescued by a fleeing neighbour, McCoy. Shortly thereafter the old woman dies, and McCoy approaches Finn at her most vulnerable to encourage her to join the IRA. 'That's a great name you've got,' he tells her. 'It's a lot to live up to.' Knowing that she blames herself for her absence during the earlier crisis and for having subsequently put her grandmother into care, McCoy uses this opportunity to remind Finn of other obligations she has failed to meet. 'You used to be very committed,' he observes. 'Are you not anymore?' Though initially she turns him down, when her relationship with McHenry ends and she finds herself homeless, orphaned, and still barely eighteen, she turns to McCoy seeking not only direction and purpose, but re-entry into the community she had left behind.[3]

To judge by her unfortunate circumstances and tortured psyche, however, Finn's return to the Republican fold does not help her heal. Moreover, Devlin's teleplay suggests that Finn's experience is representative, her own decline a consequence of the collapse of normality around her. Her symbolic function is suggested by the repeated identification of her character with Nationalist west Belfast. In response to police interrogation, for example, she recites the names of the streets off the Falls Road, a technique of non-cooperation she leaned from the IRA. 'There had been everything from birth to death on that road – once, but now gone,' she mourns, recalling the fire which destroyed her home. Years later, when she takes Kirk on a tour of the area, she can still show him nothing but 'empty and broken and beaten places,' which, as she explains to McBride, the English detective who interrogates her, are the only places she knows.

Like *The Long March*, *Naming The Names* suggests that sinister forces behind the scenes orchestrate Republican violence and lure the weak and directionless to support and take part in it by promising to fill a void in their lives. In normal, happy people, that space is already full with friends, family, a career, ambitions – in short, with all the positive, creative activities open to the grounded and the sane. That violence is incompatible with traditional forms of contentment is, of course, a familiar theme. Although Helen is a chronic bungler, and although the extent of Finn's psychosis may be explanation enough for her destructive effect on others, as John Hill has observed in his analysis of cinematic images of the conflict in Northern Ireland, those who are drawn to violence in pursuit of political ideals surrender the right to love and live in peace.[4] Helen never really learns this lesson; Finn learns it too late. Only Mona seems to take it to heart, and to accept as the price of political commitment the subsumation of all other aspects of her personality.

As a consequence of this bargain, Mona is emotionally frigid, a not unusual temperature for Irish Republican women in film and television drama. When Helen's father refuses to support the Hunger Strike, it is Mona who leads the angry mob which threatens to burn him out. Unmoved by reason or compassion, she even ignores the local priest who begs her to consider the consequences of her actions, and to ask herself why 'anyone would willingly support a government run by you when you stoop to these methods.' Though she does back down

eventually, her decision reflects no change of heart. 'We go because we choose to go and not because you said to,' she tells the priest defiantly as the crowd disperses, leaving Helen's mother, the victim of a Loyalist arson attack ten years earlier, no less terrorised than she had been then.[5]

Because her characterisation stresses her inhumanity, Mona's gender is in one sense irrelevant – hence her passionless union with Colm, a man who by his own description finds intolerance attractive and places compassion beneath contempt.[6] Though Helen is struck by Mona's delicate features and dramatic colouring, Colm claims indifference to her beauty: to him, Mona is attractive because she is 'incorruptible,' because 'she puts her politics first,' and because her commitment is 'so total and unrelenting.' To underscore the aridity of their union, Colm goes on the run almost immediately after they marry, and when the inevitable news of his death reaches her, Mona accepts it apparently without grief.[7]

Though Devlin implicitly rejects her politics by depicting her as unfeeling and cold, Mona's commitment to the Cause is indisputable. In *Naming the Names*, by contrast, politics functions purely as foreplay. Finn and McHenry argue briefly about the media's coverage of the looting of a Protestant shop, but the discussion takes place in bed and soon is abandoned for other pursuits.[8] The same pattern emerges when she takes up with Kirk. His description of his doctoral thesis – that Protestant opposition to a united Ireland was a reasonable response to the threat of discrimination in an overwhelmingly Catholic state – sends her into an apoplectic rage whose ferocity is especially startling against the backdrop of the library in which the scene takes place. 'You get angry very quickly,' Kirk observes; 'who's done that to you, Finn?' His question only provokes her further, which drives him to despair ('Oh how did I get into this!'), and yet when she storms out he follows, and though this is only their second encounter he accompanies her back to her flat, where they make love. Politics is not mentioned by either of them again.

Political debate can be an aphrodisiac in *The Long March* as well, but it is more frequently used as a means of avoiding or redirecting

interpersonal conflict among characters whose personalities are habitually opposed. 'You know your problem, Joe?' Helen's mother tells her husband in the wake of a heated, ostensibly political disagreement between him and Helen. 'She's too like you.' Elsewhere discussion degenerates into the airing of long-standing personal grievances, as when Helen responds to her mother's objections to her support for the Hunger Strikers as if she personally were under attack: 'Just once,' she says, 'it would be nice to know there was something about me you approved of.' Also telling is the explanation she offers for her parents' frosty reception of Michael, another old friend from her CRM days. 'Airy Neave's been murdered,' Helen tells him as they leave the house. 'There's also the fact that my sister's getting married next month, I've left my husband, and you and Fergus Sloan and the Civil Rights Marchers are responsible for all our troubles. But the real trouble is' – and here she stops and faces him – 'my father is never at home.'

IMPLICATIONS

In representing their support for a united Ireland as an emotional response to personal crisis, teleplays such as Devlin's belittle their protagonists as political actors, further disempowering them within an already oppressive system. Moreover, by making their 'heroines' into victims and dupes, such narratives contribute to the delegitimisation of an ideology to which many women have lent their support.

This is particularly true of *Naming The Names*. Driven by her appetites and the figments of her disturbed imagination, Finn makes a poor representative for Northern Irish nationalism, particularly when her depiction is contrasted with that of the other principal characters in the narrative – all of whom are English. 'The problem with you is you're improbable,' Kirk tells her with fond condescension, 'and sometimes I think you live in a dream.' McHenry describes her affectionately as 'a wee lunatic;' 'That's what everybody says,' she sighs. Her lunacy soon proves destructive, however. She torments McHenry incessantly with accusations of infidelity and makes unreasonable demands for his attention to the detriment of his work.[9] 'I feel as if

you're taking my life away from me!' she wails during one public confrontation at the height of the Ulster Workers Council Strike. To all this McHenry responds with super-human patience, but the emotional disorders from which Finn suffers are fatiguing, unpredictable, and impossible to control. In one scene he wakes her from a nightmare and she pleads with him to hold her hand; moments later she insists he release her, only to scream hysterically when he does. When he is brought to the police barracks to see her towards the end of the drama, she accuses him of desertion when in fact it was she who left him, and she blames him for her subsequent decline. 'He never challenged me, never asked me why,' she complains to the detectives, but given the evidence, the viewer's sympathies can only lie with him.[10]

Similarly, the darker aspects of Finn's personality are underscored by the gentle, trusting nature of her victim, an Oxford-educated intellectual whom Finn herself admits can not be held responsible for any aspect of the conflict in the North. Seduction and betrayal, symbolised by the spider's web which appears throughout the drama, are, it's implied, essential to the Republican arsenal, and in *Naming The Names* are deployed against a cast of British characters who are uniformly good-hearted, patient, and sincere. Of course, Finn herself is caught in a web by McCoy and his cohorts, who exploit her weaknesses and teach her to use her body not for the creative purposes for which it was designed but in the service of death. It is this unnatural act which is depicted as the most reprehensible aspect of her crime. Her ability to tell Kirk that she loves him just moments before she lets him be killed visibly horrifies McHenry. 'In God's name, Finn,' he shudders. 'You caused the death of someone you had grown to know, cold-bloodedly led a young man to his killers. And you made friends with him first!'[11]

By juxtaposing a deranged and destructive Northern Irish woman with an array of kindly, sensible English men, *Naming The Names* implies that England itself is fundamentally different from the North.[12] *The Long March* supports the same conclusion. It is in England that Helen approaches self-realisation; it is there that her friend Michael weds his girlfriend and that Sloan and his wife are finally able to repair their marriage (which his former affair with Helen had all but destroyed). England is 'another world,' a place for fresh starts and reconciliations; Northern Ireland, by contrast, is stuck in the past. 'You forget how suffocating this place can be,' Helen observes, a sentiment later echoed by Colm, who, despite his obvious love for his country, admits, referring to Belfast, that '[t]his town depresses me sometimes.'

It is not surprising in light of this comparison that *The Long March*, like *Naming The Names*, effectively absolves the British Government of any responsibility for the violence in the North. When, for example, Helen accuses 'the British' of deliberately provoking civil unrest by refusing to negotiate with the Hunger Strikers, her father (a committed socialist and trade union activist and a highly sympathetic character) replies that it is the IRA who have prolonged the protest by rejecting the Government's offer of prison reforms; earlier, Devlin has him remind his daughter that shortly before he was murdered, Airey Neave had publicly promised to end the interrogation centres if the Conservatives came to power. In short, it is the Republicans' own actions which are to blame for the conditions by which they feel oppressed, making their violence both illogical and unnecessary.

Shortly before *The Long March* concludes, Sloan describes a recent verdict by the European Court of Human Rights, which, having considered Republican demands for special category status, 'agreed entirely with the British authorities.' What decided the issue for the Court, Fergus explains,

> was that [the Republicans] haven't defined any beliefs such as agnosticism or pacifism. 'Belief' is the key word in Article 9 [which outlines the right to freedom of thought, conscience and religion, including the right to change one's religion or beliefs]. The British authorities argued that [the term] 'belief' in Article 9 relates to the holding of a philosophy or spiritual conviction which must have an identifiable form and content. It does not extend to a deeply held feeling, which they call 'opinion'.

Coming from a respected, independent adjudicator, the Court's decision not only rejects the right of convicted Republicans to be

treated as political prisoners, but reduces to a mere 'opinion' the very foundation of their ideology and the historical vision out of which it evolved.

VICTIMS NO MORE:

Orla Walsh's *The Visit*

Like the 1985 Anglo-Irish Agreement before it, the Downing Street Declaration signed by John Major and Albert Reynolds in 1993 marks a significant change in Britain's official agenda for the North. Although offered within the context of an unequivocal condemnation of violence and the firm reiteration that the ultimate responsibility for the socio-political future of the North lies as ever with the Northern Irish themselves, this document validates the Nationalist-Republican tradition by explicitly acknowledging the historical roots of the conflict (and, in so doing, its intrinsically political nature), and by accepting at least partial responsibility for current divisions and tensions in the North.

In keeping with these developments, teleplays produced from the late 1980s on have presented a much more complex picture of Irish nationalism than do the narratives discussed so far. Among the first to challenge conventional representations of the Nationalist-Republican experience in the North was *Hush-A-Bye Baby* (C4, 1990), the story of a fifteen-year-old Catholic from Derry who discovers she's pregnant soon after her boyfriend's arrest.[13] Less well-known is Tom McGurk's teleplay *Dear Sarah* (ITV, 1990), which focuses on Sarah Conlon's efforts to free her husband, Giuseppe, one of the 'Maguire Seven' wrongly convicted of terrorist crimes.[14] Unlike Ken Loach's 1993 feature film about the Conlons, *In The Name of The Father*, which largely ignored the complex relationships responsible for anti-Irish racism in Britain and the patterns of injustice which are its consequence, *Dear Sarah* exposes these forces through its story of an ordinary family transformed by events over which they have no control.

This trend away from the simplistic and the narrowly personal has continued with the production of teleplays directly concerned with the experience of the Nationalist movement in the North, and with the diverse constituencies which that movement represents. To illustrate this evolution, I have chosen two short dramas featuring female protagonists, both of which aired as part of Channel 4's 1994 series, *The Long War*.[15] The first of these, 'The Visit,' written and directed by Orla Walsh, is one of a growing number of television dramas which explore the lives of Republican prisoners and their families.[16] Drawn from a story published in a prisoner's magazine by Lawrence McKeown, Walsh's drama depicts through flashbacks the reflections of a woman on her way to visit her husband, a Republican prisoner in a Northern Irish jail.[17]

Sheila and Sean are only recently married when he is arrested and sent to prison in the first days of Internment. As a prisoner's wife, Sheila is accorded a form of respect which proscribes even the most innocent overtures by other men and depends on her remaining forever chaste: at least one woman we hear who shares Sheila's status has been tarred and feathered for infidelity. The resulting isolation is especially burdensome for Sheila, whose marriage was too brief to have borne fruit. Whereas other wives of Republican prisoners have children to occupy their time and attention, Sheila returns to an empty house. Nor can she turn for support to her family, by whom she's been largely disowned because of her marriage. 'Your father doesn't know I'm seeing you,' her mother tells her coldly when they meet, apparently for the first time in ages. 'You better not call me.'

Roughly fifteen years pass between Sean's arrest and 1987, when the drama is set.[18] Though she's well aware of the risks involved, Sheila begins an affair with a fellow teacher at the Irish-language school where she works. When she becomes pregnant, her lover, Mallory, proposes to support her and the child. 'If you're serious about keeping it,' he offers, 'maybe I could get a transfer back down to Dublin, we could get a house. No one would bother us there.' But Sheila doesn't want to escape her circumstances; she simply wants to improve them. 'I'm not leaving my home, or Sean,' she replies hotly. 'I stood by him through it all. Now I'll see if he has the strength to stand by me.'

Although Sheila clearly intends from the outset to abandon Mallory

as soon as he's played out his part in her plan, if she seduces him it is in order to create a new life and to resurrect her own, not to destroy his. Unable despite her loss to mourn for her husband because he is still very much alive, and unable to divorce or leave him even if she wanted to for fear of the consequences, this unusual solution to her dilemma is, it's implied, the only one available to her. That she doesn't want to leave Sean, however, defines her affair as a political act.

'You get to feeling sexy around death,' Sheila tells Mallory, shortly before they first make love. 'Not because it turns you on, but because you fear death, and the only way to be alive is to be with someone, to make love.'[19] By transforming the role of life-giver from passive to (pro)active, Walsh's teleplay redefines values traditionally associated with women in the midst of violent conflict. Thus Sheila's actions can be read as a form of protest, and not only against the prevailing stereotype of women as long-suffering martyrs to their husbands' and lovers' political ideals. In challenging the rules of strict loyalty which protect the interests of Republican men whatever the consequences for the women (and children) on whom they're imposed, Sheila also defies the oppressive system which she and Sean and other Republicans hold responsible for their circumstances, whether in prison or back home.

Evidence of this oppression is everywhere. The teleplay opens with images of Belfast, like the statue of Queen Victoria outside City Hall, which establish the British Government's hold on the city and imply the Unionists' political clout. A flashback reveals the trauma of Sean's arrest, conveyed most sharply by Sheila's screams as her husband is dragged from their bed. On her way to the prison shuttle Sheila passes barricades, security cameras, police patrols and leering soldiers. Arriving at the prison after a long and uncomfortable journey, she and Sean endure only brief, impersonal meetings with no opportunity for intimacy, surrounded by No Touching signs and wardens positioning themselves nearby. Back in Belfast graffiti promises Our Day Will Come, and an inscription accompanying a gable-high portrait of Bobby Sands declares, 'Everyone, Republican or otherwise, has his part to play.'[20] Sheila's decision to take a lover and bear his child while remaining loyal to her husband can be seen as a redefinition of the role that had been assigned to her. Moreover, by rejecting the promise of new life in Dublin, she reaffirms not only her love for Sean (which, despite the years of separation and her family's objections, remains undiminished), but her support for the Cause to which he's devoted his life.

162

Sheila's courage and determination reflect well on all Republicans, including those prisoners with whose harsh conditions of confinement Sheila's own restrictive lifestyle is implicitly linked. Furthermore, the narrative's verbal and visual allusions to the dirty protests and hunger strikes through which Sheila has 'stood by' her man enlarge the significance of their relationship beyond that of husband and wife, so that the tensions which challenge their marriage come to mirror those between feminism and the Republican movement. This is of course a subject with which Devlin's work also has been concerned. The experience of her heroines, however, suggests that those tensions are irreconcilable. The most liberated of her female characters reject the conventions of Republican ethnicity and may even abandon the North, while her weaker protagonists, like Helen Walsh, are moved less by political conviction than by the men who overpower their hearts. Helen's first thought when Colm leaves her, for example – 'What am I to do now?' – exposes the emptiness of her commitment to the Republican cause. Elsewhere she confesses that even at the height of her involvment in the Civil Rights Movement, the affair she was having with Sloan at the time was more important to her than achieving justice. In Walsh's drama, by contrast, Sheila's love for Sean is simultaneously personal and political, implying a definition of Freedom which can include both her struggle and his.[21]

'The Visit' ends without resolution. The final image is of Sheila, pale and serious, framed in the doorway of the room where her husband is eagerly waiting, unaware of the news she is about to break; moreover, the image concludes a narrative which confines to flashback all significant dialogue, so that the Sheila of the present is an anxious and silent character who spends most of her time on screen alone with her thoughts. Nevertheless, Walsh implies, the prospects for the future are not necessarily bleak. In affectionately describing her husband as 'a

great dreamer' who in his youth was 'always making plans, mad plans,' Sheila suggests that Sean (and through him, Republicanism) may have imagination enough to embrace her needs, so that love, life, and Republican politics need not be at odds.

163

VALIDATING THE NATIONALIST TRADITION:
Stephen Burke's *After 68*

While 'The Visit' is remarkable for its depiction of men and women unequivocally committed to the Republican tradition of protest and resistance, 'After 68,' like *Hush-A-Bye Baby* and *Dear Sarah*, is concerned with the experience of Northern Catholics whose support for militant nationalism is ambivalent, if not openly hostile. Written and directed by Stephen Burke, 'After 68' revisits the inception of the Troubles in Derry through the eyes of its narrator, Freda, the illegitimate daughter of a Catholic woman and a married Protestant man.

In 1968, Freda is a typical teenager preoccupied with boys and clothes and the latest in pop music, but kept sensible through the influence of a strong and loving parent. Though Freda herself is largely oblivious to the socio-political turmoil which is fomenting around her, her mother joins in the first demonstrations of the Civil Rights Movement, exhilarated by the spirit of solidarity among the protesters. Gradually, however, her optimism fades. Though at first she hails the arrival of the British army as 'a victory' for Nationalists and for all those seeking justice, the events of Bloody Sunday shock and sicken her, and she decides to leave Derry with her daughter and wait out the Troubles in Donegal. The move is intended to be only temporary, but apart from one brief and difficult visit after the death of her father, Freda and her mother never return.

In keeping with the influence of politics on the personal drama it portrays, 'After 68' is montage of fictional scenes intercut with black-and-white footage of actual demonstrations, confrontations, and other events from the early years of the conflict in the North. The script is strictly factual, a record primarily of historical events, e.g., 'The long march from Belfast to Derry was based on the Black Civil Rights march from Selma to Montgomery in Alabama.' Elsewhere, key socio-political developments are linked with their practical consequences for Freda and her mother, for example, 'The barricades went up again. I was grounded.'

Apart from this narrative voice-over, no other speech is heard or shown; instead, the characters communicate silently, through facial expression, gesture and touch. The absence of conventional dialogue enhances the power of the visual imagery, and focuses the viewer's attention less on character than on the chronology of events: stones are thrown at the Civil Rights Marchers and Freda's mother returns home bruised; the army arrives to protect the Catholics and her mother's hopes for change are renewed; the B Specials are replaced by the Ulster Defence Regiment and her father, a former Unionist representative to the City Council, becomes a part-time volunteer.

Through both form and content, Burke's drama captures not only the mass and momentum of history in the North, but also the concurrence of individual stories which the outbreak of the Troubles may have muted, but never managed to overwhelm. 'After 68' is therefore a testament to the courage and resilience of the many, then and now, who have struggled to lead 'normal' lives within and despite a culture of violence. It is also a refreshing departure from more conventional narratives which continue to exploit Northern Ireland as a backdrop for tales of revenge, political intrigue, or the cataclysmic consequences of sectarian conflict. By creating characters with whom identification is both inviting and easy, Burke's teleplay validates a tradition of protest of which contemporary Northern Nationalism is justly proud, and, in so doing, legitimises the grievances which fuel that protest even now.

A generous reader might argue that *Naming The Names* likewise sought to reveal the sources of Nationalist rage and despair by depicting the destruction of the Lower Falls, and, through Finn, the traumatic experiences of a community. But Finn is such an unreliable witness that despite the obvious depth of her suffering, identification with her cause is virtually impossible. Freda, however, is so reassuringly sane that she might have been created deliberately to offset the

influence of protagonists such as Devlin's on popular perceptions of the North.[22] The differences between the two characters reflect an essential difference in the artistic vision of their creators. Devlin's conviction that Northern Ireland sank into madness following the violence of 1969 is well-documented, and her protagonists are frequently afflicted with emotional disorders meant to symbolise this decay. Walsh's teleplay, by contrast, depicts the same historical moment not as the onset of an irreversible disease but as a difficult period of change and opportunity, whose challenge is not only to escape the tide of sectarian violence, but also to resist despair. Of the two, the latter may be the more difficult, as Burke's teleplay reveals. Although Freda and her mother escape injury, their survival does come at a price. 'I think my mother felt guilty for walking out on her friends,' Freda says, reflecting on her mother's decision to leave the North. 'After 68' thus conveys the enduring sense of loss, guilt, and regret experienced by so many of those caught up in such conflicts over their inability to prevent disaster.

165

And yet, despite the dangerous environment in which she comes of age, Freda remains well-adjusted, durable, and good-humoured. Moreover, she is one of several complex female characters whose behaviour defies expectation but not belief. Though her father is largely removed from her life and never appears on screen, Freda refers to him without resentment, nor does she imply any bitterness towards him on her mother's part, even when the outbreak of violence puts a stop to his contributions to his daughter's support. When his wife crosses a divided city shortly thereafter to see the child her husband fathered more than fifteen years before, he does not object, nor does the meeting provoke recriminations of any kind. Instead, a bond develops between the three women, and Mrs. Craig soon becomes a welcome and regular visitor to Freda's home. These visits continue until the violence comes dangerously close (a soldier is shot at the end of their street); soon after they stop Freda's mother decides to leave Derry. When her father and another UDR man are killed on patrol, however, Freda and her mother return to the city to comfort his widow, just as she had shared in their anguish earlier, when violence ripped through the Catholic community.

While in Derry for the funeral, Freda and her mother return to the house where they used to live, which is now home to squatters. There they rescue a few mementoes from the heyday of the Civil Rights Movement, including a snapshot of her mother just after a march, weary but cheerful and full of hope. Unlike Helen's in *The Long March*, however, their nostalgia is wistful but aware: neither Freda nor her mother have any doubt that 'Those days [are] gone.' The final frames of the drama capture Freda's receding view of an IRA checkpoint, its sentry hooded and heavily armed, as she and her mother drive away from the city for the last time.

CONCLUSION

The project of validation with which 'The Visit' and 'After 68' are engaged embraces both the political ambitions of the Nationalist movement and key aspects of its social agenda. That Sheila teaches the Irish language to the very young, for example, and that she is joined in this endeavour by a colleague from the South, affirms the contention that to learn the language is not simply to make a political statement, but to celebrate an essential aspect of pan-Irish culture. Likewise, in 'After 68,' when Freda enrolls in a Catholic school following the move to Donegal, she notes wryly that once again her teachers were nuns: 'Some things I couldn't escape.' Despite its irony, the remark does suggest a continuity of culture and experience between the North of Ireland and the Free State which the Border can neither disrupt nor obscure.

This celebration of Irish culture is part of a broader reclamation of outlook and objective achieved by rejecting the desperate analysis of earlier teleplays whose protagonists simply gave up on the North. For if Northern Ireland is irredeemable, as it so often is, for example, in Devlin's work, then the only options for its inhabitants are immigration and death. Moreover, many of those characters who choose the former fail to assimiliate in their new surroundings because they are unable to completely let go of the past; others find that the past refuses to let go of them. In *Lost Belongings* (ITV, 1986), for example, Stewart Parker's heroine Deirdre is lured back from a safe and

happy life in England to miscarry and die on the steps of a church in the North. In 'The Visit,' by contrast, Sheila literally brings new life into the prison where her husband will spend the better part of his, and no character in either Walsh's or Burke's drama even considers the option of escaping to England.[23]

167

The policy of abandonment so often espoused in earlier teleplays ignores the fact that those most troubled by violence in the North are often the least able to escape. Moreover, it implies that even reform, let alone revolution, is an impossibility, a conclusion which perpetuates disempowerment and which keeps individuals and communities from taking charge of their lives. For women, this effect is exacerbated by their apparent insignificance relative to men: though the focus of this essay might suggest otherwise, most female characters in these early dramas play minor roles. Furthermore, they typically are preoccupied with non-political concerns (e.g., the private, the inter-personal, the domestic, the romantic), and yet remain largely uncritical, passive, observer-recipients of the socio-political horrors that evolve around them and so often put their lives, their homes, and their loved ones at risk.

Such representations are far from realistic. Despite their virtual invisibility in electoral politics and particularly in the decision-making structures of the political parties in the North, women are committed, active members of political parties at the grassroots level, and are active in the local electoral arena as councillors.[24] Moreover, women of all political colours in Northern Ireland 'have become increasingly involved in part-time adult education; local women's groups; women's education; networking activities; [and] community development,' taking advantage of government and trust funding initiatives which have led to a strong, disparate voluntary sector and a resurgence of community-based activism.[25]

The most recent dramatic work for television has sought to reflect these realities through greater complexity of plot and character, the validation of a previously disprivileged culture and community, the repoliticisation of history and individuals, and the movement away from story lines and imagery which suggest that Northern Ireland is at all levels a place of stasis, corruption and death. Observing these changes it is tempting to imagine that a new era has begun for British television, in which the medium will at last be free to reflect perspectives which conflict with the Government's official view. The relative absence of stories which explore the complexities of Protestant identity, however, suggests that television is still being used to influence public opinion both within and outside Northern Ireland, and to solicit consent for the Government's plans for the future of the state.[26] That agenda now appears to favour unification, achieved in part by the erosion, whether through inattention or explicit dismissal, of the identification of Northern Protestants with Great Britain. Given the strengths of both Burke's and Walsh's work, for example, it is unfortunate that the third teleplay in *The Long War* series strives for humour by lampooning Loyalist culture. Written by Marie Jones, whose stage play, *A Night In November*, expressed similar themes, 'Wingnut and the Sprog' describes the unreliable Wingnut's efforts to support his illegitimate child (the 'sprog' of the title) by minding a mutt for a Loyalist thug. Pressed by a more intelligent friend to name even one aspect of Protestant culture that 'any right-minded Fenian would want' any part of, Wingnut can think of nothing but Rangers Football Club, which, as his chum reminds him, is more than matched by the Nationalist team, Celtic. It is disappointing that sandwiched between two teleplays which so imaginatively and effectively challenge stereotypes of Northern Nationalists is a drama which fails in what should have been an equivalent aim: to demonstrate that the stories of Northern Protestants are as powerful as those of any other group who has lived and died through the Troubles.

An enduring ambition of the feminist movement has been to unite women with diverse backgrounds and identites by advocating a view of the female experience which transcends divisions of race, class, ethnicity, or creed. In this view, 'The Visit,' though clearly concerned with tensions within the Republican movement, could be the story of any childless woman in the North left in limbo by the incarceration of her husband. Such commonalities are subtle, however, and may not be readily perceived. As Eilish Rooney has observed, one should not

assume that sisterhood is transcendent, particularly in the North: 'The lives of women in the North of Ireland cannot be isolated, either theoretically or practically, from their socio-economic, political or cultural contexts. Nationalist women and Unionist women will have different analyses and different experiences of the political conflict. They will have different expectations and aspirations about the future. These differences will not be less keenly disputed because the parties to the dispute are women.'[27] The challenge for writers in Northern Ireland, then, is to imagine and articulate individual experiences which have broad implications for society, community, and conceptions of justice, and which lead their viewers to reconsider their perceptions of themselves and others, even if ultimately they choose not to revise. Surely the lesson of 'The Long War' is that no complex political situation can be resolved by simply ignoring the aspirations or vision of its participants, any more than it can be explained in terms of dementia, delinquency, or romantic impulse.

In Burke's drama, there are good people on both sides of the conflict whose efforts to bridge the divisions which threaten their future are thwarted by events too momentous to ignore. Nevertheless, the two communities are closely linked, so much so, the absence of dialogue implies, that at least some relationships can transcend language. It is not insignificant, for example, that Freda's mother gives up on Derry only after her tie to the city's Protestant community is destroyed, as if only through such couplings between Catholics and Protestants can chaos be averted.

Like feminism, Republican ideology has maintained a formal commitment to inclusive politics and to the creation of a new society in which all are welcome and able to participate. Men and women within these movements must hold their representatives accountable to this rhetoric if the future of Northern Ireland is to be truly peaceful and fully democratic, whatever its eventual form.

ENDNOTES

1 Observed from an official perspective, one could argue that such representations were necessary to quell the rise in support for the IRA following the death of Bobby Sands.

2 Since 1980, Devlin has been the predominant female teleplaywright in Northern Ireland, as well as one of the most frequently produced (and consequently best known) of all dramatists concerned with the North whose work has appeared on British television. According to Rosemary Clarke, BBC Production Assistant, of the thirty-four teleplays produced by the BBC (NI) Drama Department between 1980 and 1990, no less than half were written by either Anne Devlin, Graham Reid, or Bernard McLaverty (correspondence, 1991). It is because of Devlin's popularity among producers, viewers, and (feminist) critics alike that I have chosen to use her work to illustrate the prevailing imagery of Republican women in the 1980s.

3 In her discussion of the short story from which Devlin adapted the teleplay of *Naming The Names*, Catherine Shannon has argued that Finn personifies 'the confluent pressures of political allegiance, communal loyalty and personal indebtedness for past protection' which 'enabled the Provisional IRA to gain greater support among young people in nationalist west Belfast by the mid 1970s' (C. Shannon, 'The Woman Writer as Historical Witness: Northern Ireland, 1968–1994. An Interdisciplinary Perspective', in *Engendering History*, 1997, p.248). In the teleplay, however, the narrative focus is less on Finn's 'political allegiance' than it is on her sense of guilt and her general madness.

4 John Hill , 'Images of Violence', in K. Rockett, L. Gibbons, and J. Hill, *Cinema and Ireland*, London: Routledge, 1988.

5 By implying an equivalence between Loyalist mob violence in the late 1960s and Republican violence a decade later, Devlin underscores her antipathy for the latter, which usually fares well in such comparisons. Typically, Loyalist violence has been presented as by far the more heinous, a manifestation of naked sectarianism lacking even the pretense of a political motive. That this depiction is still the norm is evidenced by, for example, Ronan Bennett's *Love Lies Bleeding* (BBC, 1993), in which the main character, an IRA gunman, describes Loyalist 'ideology' in this way: 'That's what they do, that's what they're about. They kill Catholics.'

6 Though emotional frigidity is often coupled with cold-bloodedness in Republican characters, the implications of these traits vary with gender. In Neil Jordan's *The Crying Game* (1992), for example, Dil, whose testicles cause

Fergus such consternation, demonstrates all the traditionally feminine traits (she is faithful, loving, tender, forgiving), while Jude, as her name implies, betrays her sex by indulging in behaviour which, in terms of the representation of Republicans, is traditionally male: she is incapable of compassion, and harbours an aggressive sexual appetite independent of love and aroused by violence. While her commitment to the Cause may be genuine, Jordan's focus is less on her politics than her personality. By contrast, Joe McAndrews, the IRA man who calmly sets fire to a prison guard in Jim Sheridan's *In The Name of the Father* (1993) is depicted as 'the real thing'—i.e., in terms of his commitment – from whom the fictional Gerry Conlon claims to have 'learned a lot' about Irish history and politics, however repulsed he is, ultimately, by Joe's brutality.

7   Though Colm says he's leaving Helen to join the INLA ('I don't hate you,' he tells her as he ends their affair, 'I just don't have any time for women like you'), the proximity of his decision to his marriage to Mona implies an equivalence between the Cause and the woman, whose raven hair and alabaster skin, so reminiscent of Victorian images of Hibernia, only strengthen the analogy.

8   Finn regales the looters as 'hoodlums' and thugs, but McHenry dismisses her analysis as 'naive': 'Just because they don't share your political convictions doesn't mean they weren't politically motivated,' he chides. Like most English characters in the teleplays of this period and particularly so here, McHenry has a clarity of vision about the North which seems to elude the natives.

9   Unable to keep her own home in order, Finn later disrupts Kirk's, who, when Finn meets him, is living with another woman. Like Finn, who according to McHenry 'can't sew . . . can't cook . . . and [spends her] whole life sleeping,' Helen too refuses to conform to conventional expectations of female respectability, and as a consequence has acquired a reputation as a wrecker of other women's homes. In keeping with her character, however, Helen's efforts to entrap men are, unlike Finn's, consistently ineffectual.

10   Readers of Devlin's original short story may have a different response, however (see 'Naming The Names' in *The Hurt World: Short Stories of the Troubles*, Belfast: Blackstaff, 1995). Catherine Shannon, for example, has argued that metaphorically the story concerns the 'belated and ultimately bungled British intervention' in the North (Shannon, forthcoming, p. 217). Finn's psychosis is considerably muted in the first person, and the less broken, largely chronological written narrative makes her character seem more stable and sane. Moreover, her motivations for becoming 'involved' are more clearly political in the original, a response initially to Internment strengthened by a shoot-to-kill incident which takes place in front of her, involving the army and a well-known member of the IRA.

11 Devlin pursues a similar theme in *The Long March*. When Colm abandons Helen for the INLA, for example, she accuses him of 'using love as a disguise,' a charge he neither confirms nor denies.

12 The dichotomy between the two nations is not unique to Devlin's work. In fact, most of the teleplays produced during the 1980s reflect some variation on this theme, one of the most egregious being Stewart Parker's six-part series for ITV, *Lost Belongings* (1986). See J. Cornell (forthcoming), "'Different Countries, Different Worlds': The Representation of Northern Ireland in Stewart Parker's *Lost Belongings*" in James McKillop, ed., *Irish Cinema Reader*, Syracuse: Syracuse University Press.

13 *Hush-A-Bye Baby* was produced by Derry Film & Video (DFV), which, with funding from Channel Four, also produced *Mother Ireland*, a documentary which provokcd controversy for including an interview with Mairead Farrell, one of three IRA members to be murdered by the SAS in Gibraltar in 1988. Though *Hush- A-Bye Baby* was released as a feature-length film, its viewership increased significantly when it aired on Channel Four in 1990. It has been rebroadcast since then several times.

14 Giuseppe Conlon, who died in prison, was vindicated posthumously with the release of the 'Guildford Four,' one of whom was his son, Gerry, who served fifteen years before his own conviction was overturned. In her catalogue of censored programmes on Irish subjects (in Liz Curtis and Mike Jempson, *Interference on the Airwaves: Ireland, the Media and the Broadcasting Ban*, London: Campaign for Press and Broadcasting Freedom, 1993), Liz Curtis describes the troubled production history of McGurk's teleplay. Given the arguments presented in this paper, that description is worth quoting in full: 'McGurk originally wrote the script as a one-hour BBC drama in 1986, but the BBC rejected it. Then David Elstein at Thames TV recommissioned it as a 90minute film, bringing in Frank Cvitanovitch as director. The project then had a bumpy ride, first rejected by Thames TV's board – apparently unnerved by the *Death on the Rock* controversy in 1988—then approved by them in the autumn of 1989, only to be vetoed again a month later. Thames had by now set up a co-production deal with RTE, the Irish broadcasting company. After Thames' withdrawal, RTE tried to interest Ulster Television and Channel Four, but without success. Finally RTE took over the entire production, financing it by pre-selling it to the ITV network. The finished film was [first] shown on ITV on 2 July 1990' (p. 78), and rebroadcast in 1994.

15 The series was complemented by a number of two-minute spots collectively titled 'The Loved ones' and broadcast throughout the week that *The Long War* aired. Together reflecting all parties to the conflict, each spot featured a visual and oral biography of someone who had died as a result of the Troubles.

Photographs of the victims as children and young adults and at important or carefree times in their lives were accompanied by a soundtrack featuring the voices of those who knew and loved them, remembering their lives and their deaths. As a tribute to the terrible waste of human potential which the conflict has caused 'The Loved Ones' is among the most powerful, and is impossible to watch without tears.

173

16   Others include Ronan Bennet's *Love Lies Bleeding* (BBC, 1994) and Graham Reid's *Life After Life* (BBC, 1995). Jim Sheridan's film, *The Boxer*, continues the trend on the big screen.

17   Walsh is one of several young filmmakers whose work was introduced to American audiences at a conference on Irish Film and Media held at the Virginia Center for the Arts in May, 1996. Notable for its willingness to challenge stereotypes and confront contentious social issues, Walsh's work includes *Bent Out of Shape* (1996), about a lonely boy's friendship with a gay film buff working in a small town video store in the Irish Republic.

18   Setting this 1994 teleplay seven years earlier retroactively validates a period of intense Republican political activity which most scholars argue was misrepresented as a consequence of the Broadcasting Ban. The book by Curtis and Jempsen, cited above, is an excellent resource on this subject.

19   A generous reader might suggest that this was a theme that Devlin's teleplays sought to convey, if it weren't for the fact of Finn's and Helen's lovers and the unhappy romances of the women themselves.

20   Since the camera lingers on this image, it is worth noting the use of the masculine pronoun. Rooney and Woods have suggested that women's contributions to peace and conflict in Northern Ireland have been largely ignored because 'they are perceived, perhaps unconsciously, as bystanders in a man's war. . . . They are ignored because they are assumed to be powerless and being ignored they may be affirmed in their sense of powerlessness'. E Rooney and M Woods, *Women, Community and Politics in Northern Ireland: A Belfast Study*, Belfast: University Of Ulster, 1995, p. 3.

21   Others too have observed a rapport between feminism and Republicanism. See for example E Fairweather, R McDonogh and M McFadyean (1984), *Only The Rivers Run Free: Northern Ireland, the Women's War*, London: Pluto Press; G Meaney (1991), *Sex and Nation: Women in Irish Culture and Politics*, Dublin ; and C Hackett (1995), 'Self-determination: the republican feminist agenda,' in *Feminist Review*, No. 50, Summer 1995, pp. 111 – 116.

22   She also could have been conceived in response to Stewart Parker's unfortunate heroine Deirdre in *Lost Belongings* (ITV, 1986). Like Freda, Deirdre is the product of a union between a Catholic and a Protestant, but in keeping with the conventions of earlier teleplays, comes to a tragic end; in these narratives, mixed relationships and their issue almost invariably self-

destruct unless the couple relocates in England.

23 Though Derry's proximity to Donegal makes the move sensible, the symbolic significance of the relocation should not go unremarked. One of three counties within the historic province of Ulster excluded when the Northern Irish state was formed and the most northern of all on the island of Ireland, for many Nationalists Donegal demonstrates the absurdly arbitrary nature of the border. As a consequence it has become a popular setting for teleplays with this theme, including Shelagh Delaney's 1993 adaptation of Jennifer Johnson's novel for the BBC, *The Railway Station Man*, and Allan Cubit's 1995 BBC mini-series, *The Hanging Gale*.

24 Rooney and Woods (1995), p 60.

25 Ibid., pp 52-53.

26 For evidence of the use of the media to shape public opinion, see B Rolston, ed, *The Media and Northern Ireland: Covering The Troubles*, Milton Keynes: Open University Press, 1991; and D Miller, *Don 't Mention the War: Northern Ireland, Propaganda and the Media*. London: Pluto Press, 1994.

27 Eilish Rooney, 'Women and Local Learning: Reflections From Formative Faultines in Northern Ireland,' presented at the national meeting of the American Conference for Irish Studies, Albany, New York, April, 1997.

AMERICA FROM HERE

JERUSHA McCORMACK

H ealth Warning:
There follows in this article a series of highly irresponsible allegations.
Those who know better, and are subject to high blood pressure, faint-
ing fits, spleen, or apoplexy should not read any further. The writer will
take no responsibility for increased immigration or the noisy self-con-
gratulation of residents of the Republic. They should be reminded (as
if current events do not do so sufficiently) that their state, in all its
senses, is, even as this is written, transmuting itself into something else.

As a completely bifurcated person, having lived almost exactly half a
life in America and the other half in Ireland, I know I actually belong
in neither. Nor am I to be trusted in either. Divided loyalties can only
lead to subversion. Whatever I say about one country will comment on
the other. Whatever I do in one country will live up the stereotype of
the other. In American I am regarded as Irish. My accent broadens and
I slip into idiom, inviting people for a jar – or a chat – in a country
that drinks mineral water, goes to bed at ten, and has no time for idle
talk. In Ireland, I become American: outspoken. Standing on my
rights. Insisting, in a world conscious of constraints, on having my
choice. Ruefully, I reflect that the only place I really belong is on a jet
cruising the mid-Atlantic.

It is easy, having become Irish, to be wicked about America. America
from here is big and obvious and feels something of a bully. Here one
is always sensitive to America's power. The power of money: in the
Republic, American business is escalating exponentially. Almost daily
there are bulletins of the latest multinational opening a new factory.

From Captain America's to McDonalds to Planet Hollywood, American fast food has revolutionized downtown Dublin. The Coca-Colonization of the Republic has taken over the media, advertising, and much of Irish business values.

And in America – in turn – the small, cozy, arty Republic has become indecently fashionable. The latest Irish novels are in Manhattan book-stores. A 'lost' Irish writer (such as Maeve Brennan), who lived her last years haunting the ladies' toilet of *The New Yorker* -for which she once famously wrote her Dublin stories – is now the talk of the town. Suddenly, the rich and famous wish to visit and even live here. Last summer, Meryl Streep rented the house down the road. A block away, Mia Farrow is rumoured to have bought a townhouse. Where will it all end? Where did it all go wrong? Will Ireland wind up being the latest state in the Union, after Hawaii and Alaska? What exactly is to prevent it?

For one thing, thank God, the weather. Even though American weather is full of natural catastrophes such as blizzards and tornadoes and floods, Americans feel they have a God-given right to sunshine (or at least to go to Florida). So dark, damp Ireland puts them off, even though I, in my Irish mode, know winter is far more tolerable here than, say, in Boston. Then there are the Irish habits. Drink, for instance. Americans are very afraid of a bit of the creature. One drink too many and you are on the downward road – to becoming that most dreaded of American outcasts, the derelict, the bum. This fear is very deep and codified in many ways. Public drunkenness is an offence in most American towns. One almost never, except in slum areas of large American cities, sees drunks (junkies, yes, but not drunks). Compare this to the sober citizens who stagger through the roads of Dublin Four after every International.

Fear of drink brings you the nightmare of every Irish tourist: the dry town. For those of you lucky enough not to know: the dry town is the town without a pub or a liquor store; the town which will serve no alcohol with restaurant meals. Who else but Americans could invent it? Who else but Americans would tolerate it? Who else but Americans would have even conceived of something so drastic, so utterly fascist,

as Prohibition? The great experiment in banning the sale, advertisement and manufacture of alcohol ended in abject failure. But the naive faith in the perfectibility of Human Nature persists.

Here is the great divide: it would never occur to an Irish person that Human Nature could be perfected. Quite apart from daily evidence to the contrary, the Irish have a healthy regard for the concept of Original Sin. Man is born imperfect; what otherwise is religion for? From this regard, the Irish have developed a great tolerance for human failing; a tolerance so large, in fact, that it prefers failure to whatever is its vulgar opposite, which it greets with the suspicion of a feat that defies the law of gravity. It is in the Nature of Man(kind) to be a bit slack, to make a few mistakes, sure, and drink a wee bit too much. A good man's failing.

Such slackness is a precious heritage. It should be preserved with the special ferocity usually reserved for Georgian buildings or a wood of native oak. (And, probably, one reflects, with as little success.) In Ireland there is time. Time to talk. Time to meet for lunch with friends. There exists a special time zone after midnight that is purely Irish time and is unknown in America. And, most of all, there is time after deadlines – to get the damned thing in. On time, no; but in – on Irish Time.

After more than a decade in Ireland, I realized I was no longer fit to live in America. I was late for everything - well, no, I was on time, but on Irish time. Deadlines had no meaning; they seemed as arbitrary as the times set for breakfast meetings with my colleagues. Who meets for breakfast anyway? Being at breakfast with someone is either the result of an irradicable social contract, such as marriage, or brute circumstance. Having breakfast with strangers is more in the line of a car accident than something planned – accompanied by the same feelings of bruised humanity, barely adequate for the inevitable social complexities of the situation.

But of course to me, their lives seemed like a series of such desperate improvisations. Spouses came and went – mostly went. Children were traded off for weekends or holidays. A new complex tribe emerged, the family of the ex-whatever, who gathered together, under the rubric of

177

civilization, for Christmas or summer vacation. For Americans, the relations with the ex-whatever appeared more intimate and finely-coordinated than those with the actual partner of the moment.

When my husband and I returned for three years to the States, the shocks to relicts of the Cambrian era, married for all of twenty years, were multiple. Couples with whom we had been friends since days in graduate school, now had to be visited separately, as they had split and regenerated themselves as new couples. They would describe themselves as 'moving on' and 'growing within marriage'; one couple wondered aloud if we were not stunting ourselves by remaining together. My husband would mutter darkly about the new duty to divorce. Then there were the school forms. Were our children (they enquired) biologically ours? Legally ours? And, if so, who was actually looking after them? Granny? Aunt? Step-parent or hireling? And where, in the end, and with whom did they live? I felt like some primitive life-form, filling out line after line, asserting repeatedly: our children are ours, biologically, legally; they live with us and we look after them. Obviously nothing could any longer be taken for granted as far as the American family relations were concerned.

For Americans coming to Ireland, the shock is equal. One described the experience as parachuting into Kansas in the fifties. To these blow-ins, the family seems almost the entire social world of the Irish. Those lucky enough to have Irish relations (and wish to have them) found themselves caught up in a social round of visits to cousins, great-aunts and uncles, nephews and nieces. The warmth of their greeting amazed and gratified them; as did the easy and warm acceptance of young children. In Irish suburbs, American families found their children could wander house to house, to be taken in and fed and returned, as part of a routine unknown in America for at least a generation.

On the other hand, when I first came to Ireland in the seventies, I found the absence of my own family absolutely devastating. Without knowing my family, nobody seemed to be able to locate me, except as a stranger. As I was married, but did not, as yet, have children, they wondered what I did with myself all day. The fact that I had a full-time job as a university lecturer did not register at all. When I helped set up

the local residents' association, I learned from one member (years later) that she pitied me: did I have no family, that I had to adopt the problems of a whole community to keep me busy and (by implication) emotionally fulfilled? Yet, when they came to visit, my American friends would comment on the engrossing, not to say cannibalizing nature of the large Irish family, which swallowed women whole. The small, exhausted women who survived their children would, it seemed, be drafted into being granny before they even found a remnant of a life for themselves. Pitiable perhaps to the modern American career woman; but, as one noted, a role which in America was either rejected outright or regarded as just another life-option, in Ireland is welcomed, if not always with enthusiasm, as one of life's riches.

Life's riches: for me, that is what Ireland possesses and America does not. America has a lot of things which pass as life's riches. But to sustain a family in America seems almost a miracle. To sustain friendships a prodigy. Americans are wonderful friends. They are friends quickly and usually for life. But they do not have the time, they do not have the flexibility and they often do not have the emotional sustenance themselves to see you through a crisis. Friendship is trickier in America because Americans are trained from an early age to be 'independent' - in terms of problems, to carry their own luggage. When you tell an American friend of a problem, he will try to solve it; when the problem is insoluble, such as irradicable grief, he will thank you for 'sharing the pain'. Over there, you don't share your pain; almost everyone I know in America seems to be already on emotional overload – as the logical result of not sharing their pain – and therefore cannot help anyone else bear theirs. By implication, if you are sad or stressed or stuck, you pay a professional to help you sort out your emotional 'problems'. Woody Allen script all over again, yes?

Whereas, in Ireland, because people talk, because people have time to talk, because they share their lives, each can help you to bear yours, particularly in a crisis. When my husband died suddenly – almost two years ago – I went native. His own family was originally from County Clare, so I knew something of the traditional ways, as well as the customs current in Dublin. We held a wake. One does not have wakes in fashionable Dublin Four; but ours was wonderful. News of it was spread by word of mouth. Everyone came: family, friends, neighbours, colleagues, children, old people. It helped me enormously to talk with them and, when they all went home, to have Dara there with us for the night and to say goodbye to in the morning. My American family and friends were astonished at the large Irish funeral in University Church – and then by the journey cross-country to Clare, where he was buried. That important people would take a whole day off to be with us – and then to drive all the way back to Dublin so they could work the next day, seemed prodigal to them. In America, people talk about 'investing' in friends – and the money metaphor says it all. Here there is no thought of return: Dara's colleagues and friends were with us to pay him honour, and to mark the occasion with all the generosity of spirit that they extended to him during his life.

And – of course – between the two cultures, it is death that marks the great divide. Just as Americans no longer know how to live properly, they no longer die properly. An American funeral is an hour or so long, and the congregation full of people who cannot wait to get back to work. When I came to America a few months after Dara died, no one used the word 'dead'. No one, in fact, except my family, mentioned Dara at all. They were sorry for us, but the less said the better; better all of that was buried with Dara. So it was during a visit to an Irish-American friend that I felt an explosion of relief, when he made the tea, got out the whiskey bottle, and then said: 'Right. Let's hear about the funeral.' I did not miss Ireland more than on that day.

Ireland (you see) is so good about death that, if Bord Failte got wind of it, they would market it to tourists. People – certainly the Irish-Americans – would book into Ireland for the endgame. The ads are in my mind already: 'See Dublin and die.' An all-in package holiday for family and loved ones: complete with wake, funeral and picturesque burial site.

And as soon as I think that unthinkable thought, others crowd in. Ireland is changing. Ireland, stupid Ireland, is becoming more and more Americanized. In a generation, I have seen Ireland change from a traditional society into a post-industrial one – but without any of the

intervening stages. It is not so much the fact of social change, but its speed, that is alarming; and the rate of change is accelerating. It's getting harder to find the same sense of ease, the same oxygen. Time is becoming scarcer; people more harried; better off, perhaps, but more preoccupied. Soon we too will have a harassed leisure class, with money but no time to spend it. Lunch with friends will become business lunches. Friendships will become networking; no longer entered into for their own sweet sake, but because the person could be useful to you and you to him: a kind of mutual exploitation rife in cities like Washington, DC. Work, not alcohol, will be the drug of choice. Shopping, not talking, will take up more space. Even the dread breakfast meeting has been scheduled at (of all places) my own university. Lives rich in leisure will become impoverished by money and schedules. Already my colleagues are being urged, in time-management classes, not to spend hours on the phone or in the corridors, talking with friends.

181

And what will I be doing? Probably running workshops at some well-endowed American university on 'Irish Time' or 'The Irish Way of Death' and 'Irish Decadence'. Corrupting my students into becoming something that no longer exists, that mythical person of the final years of a past century: an actual human being.

So – until it becomes transmuted into something else – here I live: in Ireland, home to Original Sin and (its logical consequence) Death; a place which still as yet accommodates the frailties the flesh is heir to. A place where family is still central. A place in which one can abandon oneself to friends. And a special space where no one expects you, ever, to be perfect.

Once when I called on a country neighbor in Clare to ask his help with my car, I commented, 'I seem to be in trouble again.' 'Sure, aren't we born to trouble and in it most of the time,' was his easy reply. How different from the jarring American insistence that all be well, that all be right, enforced by that mechanical injunction, so typically American, with which every transaction ends: 'Have a nice day.'

To which my Irish side returns: 'I have other plans, thank you.'

POETRY SECTION

Artichoke II
linocut
MARION ANDERSON

AN HISTORICAL ENGLISH ARBORETUM

RICHARD GODDEN

TENTH CENTURY

"It was al durk, an'
y think cood happen to an'
y think," the gurl rot.

Blackthorn

*Murder of King Edward
the Martyr at Corfe 978*

ELEVENTH CENTURY

Anglo-Saxon song
shafted by the Conqueror's
suffering standard.

Ash

*Killing of monks at Glastonbury
by Norman soldiers 1083*

TWELFTH CENTURY

The idea of kings
is an armed ditch: pikes, staked out,
outline the borders.

Alder

The anarchy 1135–1154

THIRTEENTH CENTURY

Displaced to footnotes
famished slaves in badlands don't
dent The Age of Faith

Chestnut

*Fulk Fitzwarin an outlaw in the
Welsh Marches; famine in the 1290s.*

FOURTEENTH CENTURY

Quercy, Bosnia:
beaten, battered by wooden
heads on nigger gates.

186

Lime

The Hundred Years War
fought mainly in France.

FIFTEENTH CENTURY

The block chops both ways,
Tiptoft topped for tailing
learned: see the wood-cut.

Elm

Execution of John Tiptoft, earl of
Worcester (bibliophile and 'Butcher')
1470.

SIXTEENTH CENTURY

Canterbury's pride
(gilded chip-board of the time)
fuels the gentry's pile.

Beech

Destruction of the shrine of
Thomas Becket in 1538.

SEVENTEENTH CENTURY

Knock, knock! *Who's there?* Charles.
Charles who? Si'down. *Where?* Sedan
and bring back old jakes.

Oak

Charles II hides up a tree after
the battle of Worcester 1651.

EIGHTEENTH CENTURY

Soil shall be sky. By
all means, through bowl and leaf
to Chippendale chair.

Walnut

England civilizes the world.

NINETEENTH CENTURY

Mahogany

The collection of plants shrubs and trees in Kew Gardens.

Trapped in metaphors
of swollen furniture, they
built with balsa cash.

187

TWENTIETH CENTURY

Deal

The First World War.

Drowned duckboards, laid End
to endless, encrypt this our
tin hat century.

EARTH

FRED JOHNSTON

"The past happened . . ."
B W BENYON: 'Brynmawr'

I

Picture this —
God dozing on a shipyard gantry
a kid taking a piss
under a football terrace
or wobbling on a two-wheeler
up an entry.

II

God said to his little Adam:
The world is at
your fingertips. Don't mess
me about.
I've perched all sorts of secrets
on your lips
put word-magic in your mouth.

III

Buttermilk dribbled
down my chin

she made a small retreat
touching my hair with her
soapy fingers, absolving sin
love went about the house
in stockinged feet.

189

IV

Minutiae of our every morning
breath over porridge
I dug my spoon
into its salty clotting
sipped hot tea
from a blue-striped mug.

V

A sort of laughing rage
our young skin crawled with it
sloped green nip-and-tuck fields
we howled through, little gods,
until the first streetlamps were lit.

VI

We lived a small life
and used small maps –
my cousins' white-gloved hands
like lillies in their laps.

VII

Am I my father's ghost?
certainly I am my mother's –
she taught me to haunt myself
in her name

lacking sisters, brothers
was I fair game?

VIII

The Sunday train to Bangor
its evangelical clank and smoke
she took my hand,
a mute perfect gesture
round the Sunday school coast
and never spoke, never spoke.

IX

Dust-angels danced in the air
descending from a cobwebbed
ceilinged heaven
she thrust a brush into those high places
brought a spidery judgement
down on her hair
turned to similar war in the kitchen.

X

Face-down, the scent of grass
and black moist earth underneath
in white gym-strip the lot of us
afternooning over hurdles, long-jump, javelins
shards of grass in our teeth.

XI

Purgatorial changing rooms
sweat, bad feet and rank underwear
Thursday's sky poignant with North Sea glooms
a shingly spatter of cold rain
on rust-wired windows
Geography: the Amazon Basin.
this new thing, *despair.*

XII

Redbrick, an apologetic tree
buildings at right-angles,
scholastic geometry
always penned you in

every morning like an orphan
unhappy, thin.

XIII

Amo, amas amat
clear-tongued singsong Latin

and Caesar galloping through Gaul
those tricky dark woods
concealing ambush

the sheer *otherness* of it all.

XIV

Always a gas-smell
a desire to twist open the taps
Bunsen burners made perfect
spear-head flames

in whispers I learned
the secondhand horrors of sex
diseases of the male genitals
and their sailory, jokey names.

XV

Biology was earthworms
dissecting the frog
the reproductive ways of rabbits
sex cloaked in a clinical fog

animals, poor things, knew not God's earthly love
and so rejoiced mindlessly
in filthy habits.

XVI

Friday evening and the Queen's Bridge men
dunchers and lunchboxes, tea-and-sugar tins
flowing round the homewards 'bus in boisterous waves
the Billys and Tommys and Alecs and Sammys of this
  world
a warm thick honey of hard work and soda bread certainty.

XVII

Beans, eggs scrambled, she'd hurried
to get the day in order
my father
behind a newspaper
while she scurried like a passionate
refugee
back and forth across some invisible border.

XVIII

A stick of shaving soap
wrapped in silver paper
his new-shaved hairs in
the immaculate sink

the smell all over
of a week drained away
the window open I looked out
on a neighbour
hanging washing on a line

sheets of white, blue, pink.

IXX

He smelled of thinners, paint
rubbed cleansing-grease
into his hands, odour of petrol

made me an ugly, too-big
cricket bat, taped the handle
terms like *wicket, runs, crease.*

XXIII

Among the ledgers and dry photographs
the Boilermakers Union yearbook
moustaches, arms crosseed, brown iron
thundering up to a brownwhite sky

ships' hulls impatient to let go
go down into history and the drowning days.

XXIV

I mitched from school into
the odour of geraniums
in brass pots never watered

an elderly spinster solidly deaf
her lady's companion shouting
that I was the wee lad from next door.

XXV

Blackout blinds still on their rollers
I watched the breadman, the Ardglass herring man
make their rounds

the peevish clack of trolleys on the overhead lines
the 'buses whimpering up the hill
the first and most primitive sounds.

XXVI

Snug in the outside toilet
I heard St Donard's bells and felt
the whole of Sunday fall like a murder

coal heaped against a whitewashed wall
when it rained the yard ran black
new shoes slopping in an oily river.

XXVII

Then I saw the fields
their quilted eloquence, climbing the hills
and what voice they had

a new language, the quarry like a bad tooth
the city below made a murmuring sound
like a child's sulk and deeply sad.

LXIII

God's asleep on Cave Hill
his face
to the welder's arc of Heaven

over the Johnstons, the Pascos
all their native sons
their Trafalgar men and linen mill women.

XLVII

His toolshed without his eagerness to work in it
gave up its bladed shine and hammer sureness

planking splintered, nails festered, both
with time became less useful and more dangerous.

L

Grass uncut in the rectangular garden
he hung out pillow cases, bed-linen

everything gone wild, a predictable riot
of yellowgreen around his knees

the single clothesline sagging when
a breeze came up, wet fabric shrouding

him, calamitous and colourful: he fought
back, pegging viciously out of love, duty.

LI

Light from somewhere touched her eyes
the lids not quite closed. I was stupified

by that casket stare, worked hard for years
to defuse it –

now memory plays chess with itself
I might have been mistaken, and if so

how can I best commemmorate you
whose ghostings were so well-timed?

those last years were the worst
before I took the train, when I had courage

to slip across your minefield mothering
into another country and wars I could handle -

back for your funeral
and that final game of staring down

you couldn't lose, I had turned inside
out, wore my heart against my skin -

the value of it all? God knows.
we went our utterly separate ways

had been doing so for years: played out
the wounding gesture, blank-eyed threat.

LII

O little god who lived
to see the sun and moon
go underground

the world was a field
and flat and playful once
now it is a lightless marsh

and mischievously round.

LIII

He drank with old men in curfewed pubs
and died with the sound of a door closing

in thick snow I found the headstone
his name not carved there, that deed forming

a sort of redemption. I clung to it -
in some secondhand manner I put things right

the earth around him seeded with the violent dead
who'd stumbled in the long Northern night.

POST SCRIPTUM

Sarah, I wish I were younger
had more guts, the old gift

not huddled in a new hunger
part lust, part anger

what sets the steadiest of us adrift –

you move now as we all did once
the chosen carelessness, the brazen nod

invisible wires suspended us and since
we've missed that on-loan arrogance

that flew us in the face of God.

LORD KELVIN'S STATUE

ROBERT GREACEN

A windy evening in June
After dinner I find a bench
In the Botanic Gardens
Near Lord Kelvin's statue.
C.P. Snow would have lauded him
For having discovered
The Second Law of Thermodynamics,
Invented a scale of temperature,
Depth-sounding apparatus, tide gauges,
A new kind of ship's compass, etc., etc.
Call him Belfast's Sir Isaac Newton
With his Order of Merit,
Burial in Westminster Abbey.

I'll bet he never agonized
Over a Magdeburg hemisphere
Like this old guy on the bench.
I don't like Kelvin's stare
As if he disapproved of me,
No dab hand at Physics.

The statue shakes his head,
Now actually speaks out loud:
'You poets are a pack of spongers
Who usually dig with the wrong foot -
You take my drift? –
Or like that Nobel rhymer
Dig with the squat pen . . . '
More followed that I didn't catch.
I was too astounded – a statue talking!
Such language from a Great Victorian!

I fled in panic to the nearest pub
There to reflect, regain composure,
Ponder on this Protestant miracle.
I ordered – naturellement –
Châteauneuf du Pape.

THE WIND SAYS

DANNY BARBARE

The
little
boat
moored
to
the
old
wooden
dock.

Life,
the
wind
says

the
lake
is
calling.

MODSOGNIR'S BORG

BEV BRAUNE

In 1050 Earl and poet, Dagazar Kerrigansson, strikes out from strife-torn Norway with a fleet of 1200 across the Atlantic for Vinland (Newfoundland). But Kerrigansson travels further than planned – southwards to the Caribbean sea. Swallowed by a colossal storm, he and survivors are shipwrecked in Muspellsheimr, Land of Fire Giants, guarded from the shores of Hel (The Under-world) by Hel's Dog, Garmr.

THE SEIGE OF GARMR'S TEETH

In that cruel cast,
 Fenris-wolf strung us
 into the giant arms
 Mother of Wolves,

caught without our ships,
into the Dragon's net,
of Angrboda,
Mountain of Grief.

On to her Back
 Fort of Shift-shapers,
 Modsognir's Borg.
 Ruler of Giants -

Was Útgarðr bolted –
shielding from the coast
The Útgarðr-Loki –
with hill-ogres rode.

Nóatun – safe port -
 the shipyard ceded,
 These giants' allies,
 fettered themselves

no longer shielded,
straddled by giants.
dwarfs of the night
to Garmr's fields.

Here alf-gifts were
of bitter sap
upon human bones.
of guarded hopes

of scattered grain
and bound inert
They too were hewn
gnawed by Garmr's Teeth.

204

So Hel greeted us
its rock-teeth bared
the Dragon, Loki
could bar our race

with The Snarling Hound -
that neither Lightning,
nor that trickster's sons
to Naastrand, Corpse-Beach.

Modsognir's Borg – Citadel of the Commander of Dark Elves
Alt-gifts – gifts created by dark elves, which first appear worthless but can be turned
into gold, e.g. dead leaves, rotting wood, wood shavings.

BOOK REVIEW

Artist's Trading Card: Otto DIx
lithograph
TERRY MORROW
TEXAS TECH UNIVERSITY

BOOK REVIEW

Fred Johnston
TRUE NORTH
SALMON POETRY, 1997 ISBN 1-897648-80-4   £5.99PB.

Fred Johnston's sixth collection of poetry, entitled *True North*, is dedicated to the memory of the poet's father, so it is appropriate that the central poems are preoccupied with establishing and exploring connections between fathers and sons. 'Shed', for instance, observes the 'bladed shine' and 'hammer sureness' of the elder man's toolshed surrender to splintering planks and festering nails, as time renders both the man and his implements 'less useful and more dangerous.' The same objective compassion allows for the achieved gravitas of 'Requiem.' Part tribute, part lament, part prayer, this poem is reminiscent of Paul Durcan's 'Glocca Morra' in the way it takes on that most difficult of subjects with unflinching directness:

> My father died quietly, without fuss
> In a room drenched with apocalyptic light
>
> His hands scrawled mad hieroglyphs on the sheets
> His claw-boned knees drew up the Mountains of the Moon
> He became a continent no sane man would explore.

Although we learn that 'he simply went away/As if the ghost of him was all there had ever been', this son is less Prince Hamlet desiring revenge than Telemachus questing after orientation and identification. Indeed, the father's metamorphosis into continent, then eternal wan-

derer – 'Latitude, longitude, we could pinpoint/The last place on earth
he'd been seen alive' – opens up Johnston's primary concern in this collection: the tension between certainty and doubt, between a sure sense
of identity and a feeling of otherness or, to use the navigational
metaphor which governs the poems, between true and magnetic north.

In the title poem, a Boxing Day walk by father and son past a local
graveyard is the occasion for the son's realization that he does not possess 'A rooting gift' but rather 'the need to let go, fall free into what
will/Absorb me, drown me.' This difference renders the sailor son (who
has clambered up through 'the rigging of my doubt') marginal, a for-
eigner to certain histories and geographies. In his universe nothing is
fixed, least of all a perspective on the home ground of Northern
Ireland:

> My True North is always shifting
> A few degrees from far off marks a considerable distance
> up close.

If this uncertainty marks the globalized individualist, post-modern
man in all his diversity and alienation, it speaks more specifically of the
experience of the 'disinherited' Northern Irish 'mixed blood', whose
composite lineage casts him as both invader and indigene, at once
British and Irish. This duality informs a number of the poems, but is
most strikingly set out in 'Two-Faced.' Here the poet describes a
Northern Irish adolescence circumscribed by geographic, linguistic and
religious divisions, a determined pragmatism and a stubborn, repres-
sive silence on the subject of history. 'Two-minded,' 'Two-cultured,'
the speaker refuses self-definition, yet laments the absence of a story:

> Even now, no one writes a word
> about that lost tribe born two-faced, we have
>
> no inheritance.

Later, a meditation on the word 'faith' leads to the confession cum declaration: 'I am always two people. There is a stone in me that cannot be
removed.'

True North is a study in contrasts and oppositions, the poet's experi-

ences and observations consistently figured as a nautical course chart-
ed between the poles of love and loneliness, romanticism and realism,
youth and age. 'Before Truth,' for instance, sets the tone for a series of
poems probing the vagaries and disappointments of love. In this vague-
ly Yeatsian lyric, the heart of an 'older man' is freed up by his love for
a 'shy girl', but once the 'secret nuts and bolts of his being' are exposed
she loses her youth and her timidity: 'No magic now, a cold sharp
logic/cuts them apart: time passes.' Apart from the obvious address of
gender difference, and the implicit lament for a lost or fading muse
(themes carried into the ensuing 'anti-love' poems), there is here a para-
ble of post-colonial crisis, a succinct imaging of that moment when the
tables turn and the slave perceives the master in all his 'shattered work-
ings.' It is a figure linked to the satirical portrait of 'Old Boaz', who
protests his lack of credit for mapping the round world – 'those who
used him fared quite well/they gave us Hiroshima, Hot Dogs and
Rock'n'Roll' – and to a companion piece 'Columbus in Galway,' which
has Columbus thinking to follow 'a map that can chart the Ocean
Sea..but not just now - I'll take my time/and let the Indies murmur in
their sleep.' This clash of lost opportunity and willed deferral bespeaks
a consciousness of history sensitive to the conditional and provisional,
to the fundamentally contradictory character of human nature.

    The dilemmas of the lover, the cartographer and the sailor are each
in their own ways metaphors for the position of the poet, whose struggle is for balance, focus and honesty. While Johnston can carry off the
kind of comic-ironic swipe effected in 'Acquiring Culture' – 'Unless
vetted first, a poet is not a very sound buy' – he is equally capable of
articulating the aesthetics of paradox that has become one of the hall-
marks of his work. As he puts it in 'Adopted Things':

> I am rooted in what's disinherited
> Something earthed
> In the unattainable.

KATHLEEN McCRACKEN

209

NOTES ON CONTRIBUTORS

HILARY BRACEFIELD is Head of Music at the University of Ulster and lectures also on the American Studies programme. She is a well-known broadcaster and critic, with interests in both classical and popular music.

DOUGLAS CARSON was born in Belfast in 1938, where he enjoyed a distinguished career in local radio and television broadcasting. Among his many interests, he is President of the Titanic Trust, and recently edited *Against the Stars*, a collection of poems about the Titanic. As author and illustrator, he is at present working on a collection of stories and drawings about Belfast in 1912, *The Titanic Indiscretions of Agnes Deay*.

JENNIFER C. CORNELL is the author of *All There Is*, which won the 1994 Drue Heinz Prize for Literature and was published in Ireland by Brandon Press in 1995. Her fiction has appeared in the 1995 *Pushcart Prize* and *Best American Short Stories* anthologies, *Phoenix Irish Short Stories 1996*, *Cabbage and Bones: An Anthology of Irish-American Women Writers*, and *The Faber Book of Contemporary Stories About Childhood*, as well as in literary journals in both the U.S. and Ireland. She teaches fiction writing, literature, and cultural studies at Oregon State University in Corvallis, where she is completing a study of the representation of Northern Ireland in British television drama.

DAVID DUBOSE comes from Lubbock, Texas. He received his BFA degree in fine art printmaking from Texas Tech University in 1986 and his MFA degree in fine art printmaking from Louisiana State University in 1990. He came to Northern Ireland in 1992 and has been the artist-in-residence at Seacourt Print Workshop in Bangor, Co Down (1993) and at Flowerfield Arts Centre in Portstewart (1994). He has lectured in Printmaking at the University of Ulster in Belfast and is currently a Director and teacher at Seacourt Print Workshop. He has exhibited his prints internationally and is included in many public and private collections.

RICHARD GODDEN is Professor of American Literature at Keele University. He has published several books of poetry as well as numerous works of literary criticism. His most recent book is *Fictions of Labor: William Faulkner and the South's Long Revolution.*

GAIL KELLY studied fine art printmaking at the Ulster College of Art and Design in Belfast and at Louisiana State University in Baton Rouge. She went on to work for Baton Rouge Arts Council in their Arts in Education programmes and taught at the Louisiana Arts and Science Center and the Talbot Center in Baton Rouge. She returned to Northern Ireland in 1992 and has continued to produce her original etchings, lithographs, woodcuts and linocuts which have been exhibited widely, both at home and abroad.

SOPHIA HILLEN KING was born and educated in Belfast and is presently Acting Director of the Institute of Irish Studies at The Queen's University of Belfast. Her research interests include the literature and cultural history of Ireland in the nineteenth and twentieth centuries. She has won several prizes for short fiction and was shortlisted for a Hennessy award in 1981. She is also the author of *The Silken Twine: A Study of the Works of Michael McLaverty* (1992) and (as editor) *In Quiet Places: The Uncollected Stories, Letters and Prose of Michael McLaverty* (1989). She co-edited *Hope and History: Eyewitness Accounts of Life in Twentieth-Century Ulster* (1996) with Sean McMahon, and is presently preparing with him a critical biography of Sam Hanna Bell, to be published in 1999.

MICHAEL LONGLEY is one of Ireland's most distinguished poets. He was born in Belfast in 1939 and worked until recently as the Combined Arts Director of the Arts Council of Northern Ireland. Among his collections are *Gorse Fires*, which won the 1991 Whitbread Poetry award, and *The Ghost Orchid* (1995). He has also published a volume of autobiography, *Tuppenny Stung*. He has enjoyed a lifelong interest in and enthusiasm for jazz.

JERUSHIA McCORMACK is Senior Lecturer at University College, Dublin, where she teaches English and American Literature. A citizen of both Ireland and the United States, her life has been divided almost exactly between the two. At present she is engaged in bringing an American Studies programme (the first of its kind) to the Republic.

MATTHEW McKEE is a graduate student at the University of Ulster at Jordanstown. He has researched and given a number of conference papers on

various aspects of Appalachian life, and is at present completing a doctoral thesis on *Cultural Identity in Southern Appalachia*.

PAUL MULDOON was born in County Armagh in 1951 and educated at St Patrick's College and Queen's University, Belfast. He is recognized as a leading figure among the younger generation of Irish poets and has published seven collections, of which *The Annals of Chile* (1994) won the T S Eliot Memorial Prize. Since 1987 he has lived in the United States, where he co-ordinates the Creative Writing Programme at Princeton University.

JANE MULLEN divides her time between Oxford, Mississippi, and Skibereen, Co Cork. She is the author of *A Complicated Situation and Other Stories* and has published a range of other short fiction. She has recently completed a novel, *The Woman of the House*, which is set in Ireland. 'Frank' and 'Mary Ellen' are extracts from a work-in-progress, *All the Old Songs*.

MAUREEN MURPHY is Professor of Secondary Education/English at Hofstra University. She is Past President of the American Conference for Irish Studies and Past Chair of the International Association for the Study of Irish Literatures, as well as being a board member of the American Irish Historical Society and the Emerald Isle Immigration Center. She has edited Maíre MacNeill's *Maíre Rua: Lady of Lemdneh*, Sara Hyland's *I Call to the Eye of the Mind* and Asenath Nicholson's *Annals of the Famine* and co-edited *Irish Literature: A Reader* and *Joyce and His Contemporaries: A Centenary Tribute*. Her current projects are two: a study of Irish domestic servants in the United States and a biography of Asenath Nicholson.

FRANK ORMSBY was born in Enniskillen, County Fermanagh and educated at Queen's University, Belfast. He is Head of English at the Royal Belfast Academical Institution and is well known as a poet and editor. He edited *The Honest Ulsterman* for many years and, as well as being an influential anthologist, has recently guest edited *Poetry Ireland*. His most recent collection of poems, *The Ghost Train*, was published by Gallery Press in 1995.

LEE WRIGHT is a full-time lecturer in the History of Art and Design at the University of Ulster. Her most recent publication is an essay on 'The Suit as a Gendered Object' for Manchester University Press. She is currently researching the issue of vernacular ideas in American Art and Design.

FRANCIS STUART
SPECIAL ISSUE

WRITING
ULSTER

NO 4
1996
£7.50

Writing Ulster No 4 is a Special Issue devoted to the work of Francis
Stuart, who in his ninety-seventh year remains one of Ireland's most
controversial writers, still capable of provoking the type of acrimonious
debate which recently erupted in the press and in literary journals.
Back copies of the issue are still available, containing articles by such
well known figures as Brendan Kennelly, Maurice Harmon, Fintan
O'Toole, Dermot Bolger, Hugo Hamilton and Medbh McGuckian, so
if you want to find out more about Stuart and his place in twentieth-
century literature, order a copy now at the special price of just £5.00.

ORDER DIRECT FROM:

  Writing Ulster, Room 12G11, University of Ulster at Jordanstown,
  Shore Road, Newtownabbey, Co Antrim, BT37 0QB, N Ireland.

Please make cheques/postal orders payable to "University of Ulster".